EDEXCEL INTERNATIONAL GCSE (9–1)

HISTORY
THE MIDDLE EAST: CONFLICT, CRISIS AND CHANGE, 1917–2012
Student Book

Hilary Brash
Series Editor: Nigel Kelly

Published by Pearson Education Limited, 80 Strand, London, WC2R 0RL.

www.pearsonglobalschools.com

Copies of official specifications for all Pearson qualifications may be found on the website: https://qualifications.pearson.com

Text © Pearson Education Limited 2017
Edited by Paul Martin and Sarah Wright
Designed by Cobalt id and Pearson Education Limited
Typeset and illustrated by Phoenix Photosetting Ltd
Original illustrations © Pearson Education Limited 2017
Cover design by Pearson Education Limited
Picture research by Sarah Hewitt
Cover photo/illustration © gettyimages.co.uk: Ullstein Bild

The rights of Hilary Brash to be identified as author of this work have been asserted by her in accordance with the Copyright, Designs and Patents Act 1988.

First published 2017

20 19 18
10 9 8 7 6 5 4 3 2

British Library Cataloguing in Publication Data
A catalogue record for this book is available from the British Library

ISBN 978 0 435 18541 1

Copyright notice
All rights reserved. No part of this publication may be reproduced in any form or by any means (including photocopying or storing it in any medium by electronic means and whether or not transiently or incidentally to some other use of this publication) without the written permission of the copyright owner, except in accordance with the provisions of the Copyright, Designs and Patents Act 1988 or under the terms of a licence issued by the Copyright Licensing Agency, Barnards Inn, 86 Fetter Lane, London EC4A 1EN (www.cla.co.uk). Applications for the copyright owner's written permission should be addressed to the publisher.

Printed in Slovakia by Neografia

Acknowledgements
The author and publisher would like to thank the following individuals and organisations for permission to reproduce photographs:
(Key: b-bottom; c-centre; l-left; r-right; t-top)

Alamy Stock Photo: Chris Hellier 38, Mike Abrahams 85, Reuters 98, 106, World History Archive 14, ZUMA Press, Inc. 27, 45, 105; Getty Images: AFP 39, Bettmann 57, 72b, Boris Spremo / Toronto Star 84, Claude Salhani / Sygma 77, David Hume Kennerly 71, DEA / W. BUSS / De Agostini 3, ERIC FEFERBERG / AFP 87, ESAIAS BAITEL / AFP 86, Frank Scherschel / The LIFE Picture Collection 25, © Hulton-Deutsch Collection / CORBIS / Corbis 12, 36, Hulton Archive 62, J. DAVID AKE / AFP 94, Jack Garofalo / Paris Match 69, James Lukoski 2, Jonathan S. Blair / National Geographic 72, KARL SCHUMACHER / AFP 74, Keystone 9, Keystone-France / Gamma-Keystone 43, 52b, Marco Di Lauro 99, Mario De Biasi Sergio Del Grande / Mondadori Portfolio 50, Mario Geo / Toronto Star 20, Peter Davis 24, Roland Neveu / LightRocket 79, Terence Spencer / The LIFE Picture Collection 46, ullstein bild 54, Universal History Archive / UIG 6; TopFoto: © 2000 Topham / Picturepoint 61, © 2002 Topham / AP 18, © ullsteinbild 10; Zaprock Productions: 52t

Inside front cover: Shutterstock.com: Dmitry Lobanov

All other images © Pearson Education Limited

We are grateful to the following for permission to reproduce copyright material:

Text
Article on page 56 from Six days in June, The Guardian, 06/05/2007 (Urquhart, C), Copyright Guardian News & Media Ltd 2017; Extract on page 103 from author correspondence with Zogi Fibert, used with permission.

Select glossary terms have been taken from *The Longman Dictionary of Contemporary English Online*.

Disclaimer
All maps in this book are drawn to support the key learning points. They are illustrative in style and are not exact representations.

Endorsement Statement
In order to ensure that this resource offers high-quality support for the associated Pearson qualification, it has been through a review process by the awarding body. This process confirms that this resource fully covers the teaching and learning content of the specification or part of a specification at which it is aimed. It also confirms that it demonstrates an appropriate balance between the development of subject skills, knowledge and understanding, in addition to preparation for assessment.

Endorsement does not cover any guidance on assessment activities or processes (e.g. practice questions or advice on how to answer assessment questions), included in the resource nor does it prescribe any particular approach to the teaching or delivery of a related course.

While the publishers have made every attempt to ensure that advice on the qualification and its assessment is accurate, the official specification and associated assessment guidance materials are the only authoritative source of information and should always be referred to for definitive guidance.

Pearson examiners have not contributed to any sections in this resource relevant to examination papers for which they have responsibility.

Examiners will not use endorsed resources as a source of material for any assessment set by Pearson. Endorsement of a resource does not mean that the resource is required to achieve this Pearson qualification, nor does it mean that it is the only suitable material available to support the qualification, and any resource lists produced by the awarding body shall include this and other appropriate resources.

ABOUT THIS BOOK	**IV**
TIMELINE	**VI**
1. BUILD-UP OF TENSION IN PALESTINE, 1917–48	**2**
2. THE CREATION OF ISRAEL, THE WAR OF 1948–49 AND THE SUEZ CRISIS OF 1956	**24**
3. TENSION AND CONFLICT, 1956–73	**43**
4. DIPLOMACY, PEACE THEN WIDER WAR, 1973–83	**69**
5. THE ATTEMPTS TO FIND A LASTING PEACE, 1987–2012	**84**
GLOSSARY	**111**
INDEX	**113**

ABOUT THIS BOOK

This book is written for students following the Edexcel International GCSE (9–1) History specification and covers one unit of the course. This unit is The Middle East: Conflict, Crisis and Change, 1917–2012, one of the Breadth Studies.

The History course has been structured so that teaching and learning can take place in any order, both in the classroom and in any independent learning. The book contains five chapters which match the five areas of content in the specification:
- Build-up of tension in Palestine, 1917–48
- The creation of Israel, the war of 1948–49 and the Suez Crisis of 1956
- Tension and conflict, 1956–73
- Diplomacy, peace then wider war, 1973–83
- The attempts to find a lasting peace, 1987–2012

Each chapter is split into multiple sections to break down content into manageable chunks and to ensure full coverage of the specification.

Each chapter features a mix of learning and activities. Sources are embedded throughout to develop your understanding and exam-style questions help you to put learning into practice. Recap pages at the end of each chapter summarise key information and let you check your understanding. Exam guidance pages help you prepare confidently for the exam.

Learning objectives
Each section starts with a list of what you will learn in it. They are carefully tailored to address key assessment objectives central to the course.

Timeline
Visual representation of events to clarify the order in which they happened.

Extend your knowledge
Interesting facts to encourage wider thought and stimulate discussion. They are closely related to key issues and allow you to add depth to your knowledge and answers.

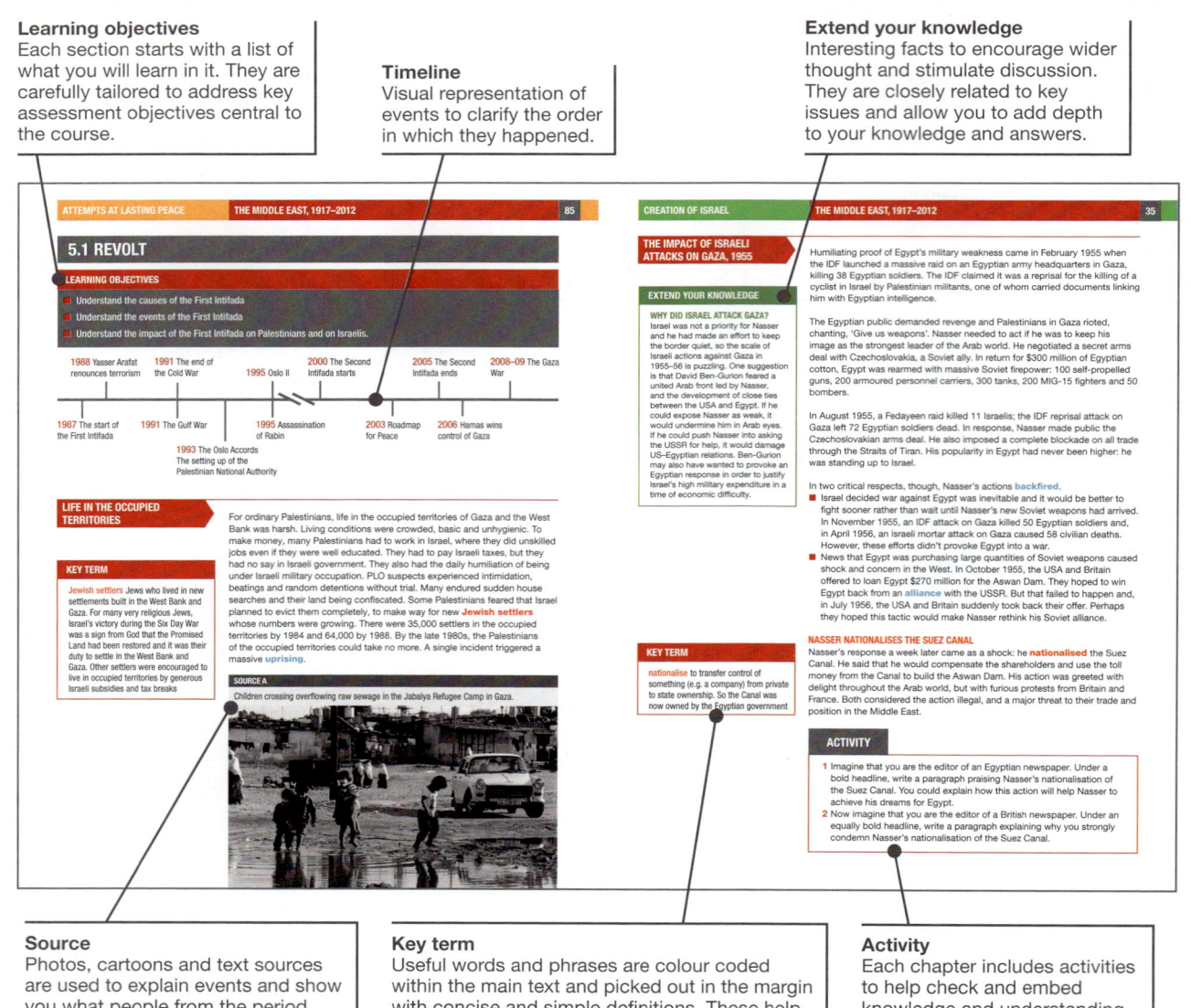

Source
Photos, cartoons and text sources are used to explain events and show you what people from the period said, thought or created, helping you to build your understanding.

Key term
Useful words and phrases are colour coded within the main text and picked out in the margin with concise and simple definitions. These help understanding of key subject terms and support students whose first language is not English.

Activity
Each chapter includes activities to help check and embed knowledge and understanding.

ABOUT THIS BOOK

Recap
At the end of each chapter, you will find a page designed to help you consolidate and reflect on the chapter as a whole.

Recall quiz
This quick quiz is ideal for checking your knowledge or for revision.

Exam-style question
Questions tailored to the Pearson Edexcel specification to allow for practice and development of exam writing technique. They also allow for practice responding to the command words used in the exams.

Skills
Relevant exam questions have been assigned the key skills which you will gain from undertaking them, allowing for a strong focus on particular academic qualities. These transferable skills are highly valued in further study and the workplace.

Hint
All exam-style questions are accompanied by a hint to help you get started on an answer.

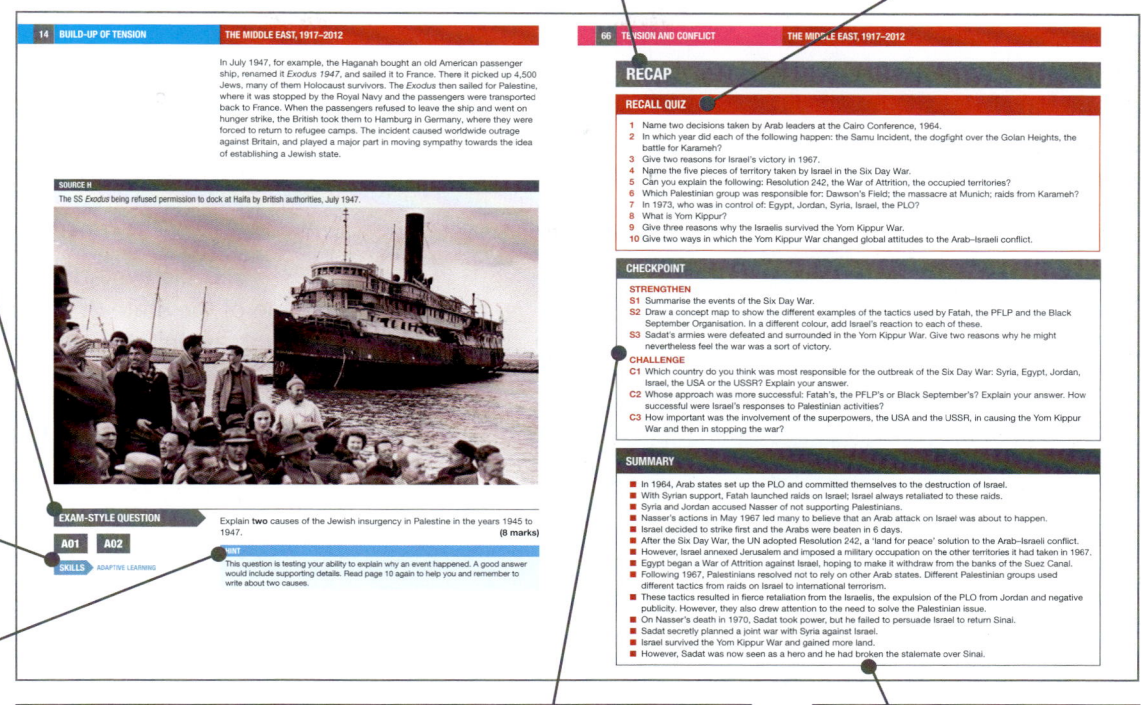

Checkpoint
Checkpoints help you to check and reflect on your learning. The Strengthen section helps you to consolidate knowledge and understanding, and check that you have grasped the basic ideas and skills. The Challenge questions push you to go beyond just understanding the information, and into evaluation and analysis of what you have studied.

Summary
The main points of each chapter are summarised in a series of bullet points. These are great for embedding core knowledge and handy for revision.

Exam guidance
At the end of each chapter, you will find two pages designed to help you better understand the exam questions and how to answer them. Each exam guidance section focuses on a particular question type that you will find in the exam, allowing you to approach them with confidence.

Student answers
Exemplar student answers are used to show what an answer to the exam question may look like. There are often two levels of answers so you can see what you need to do to write better responses.

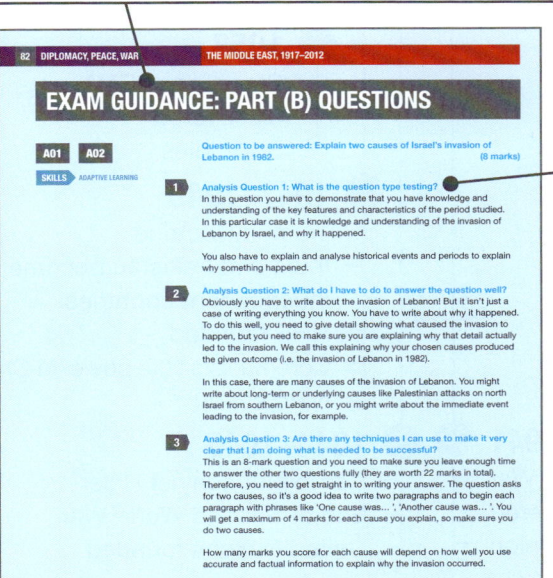

Advice on answering the question
Three key questions about the exam question are answered here in order to explain what the question is testing and what you need to do to succeed in the exam.

Pearson Progression
Sample student answers have been given a **Pearson Step** from 1 to 12. This tells you how well the response has met the criteria in the **Pearson Progression Map**.

Commentary
Feedback on the quality of the answer is provided to help you understand their strengths and weaknesses and show how they can be improved.

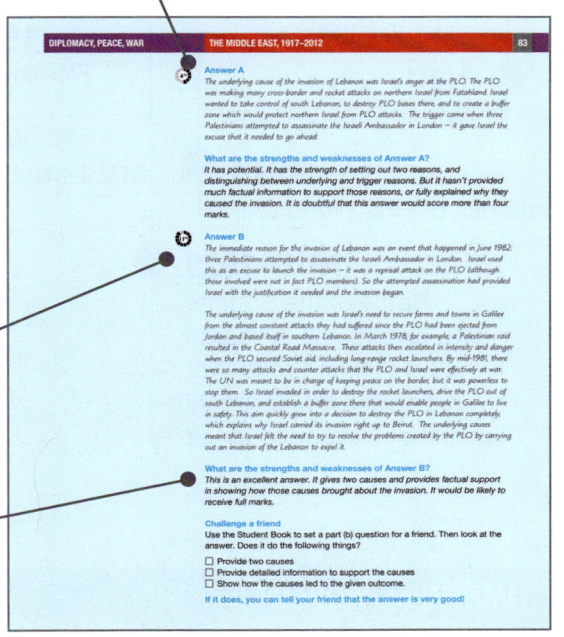

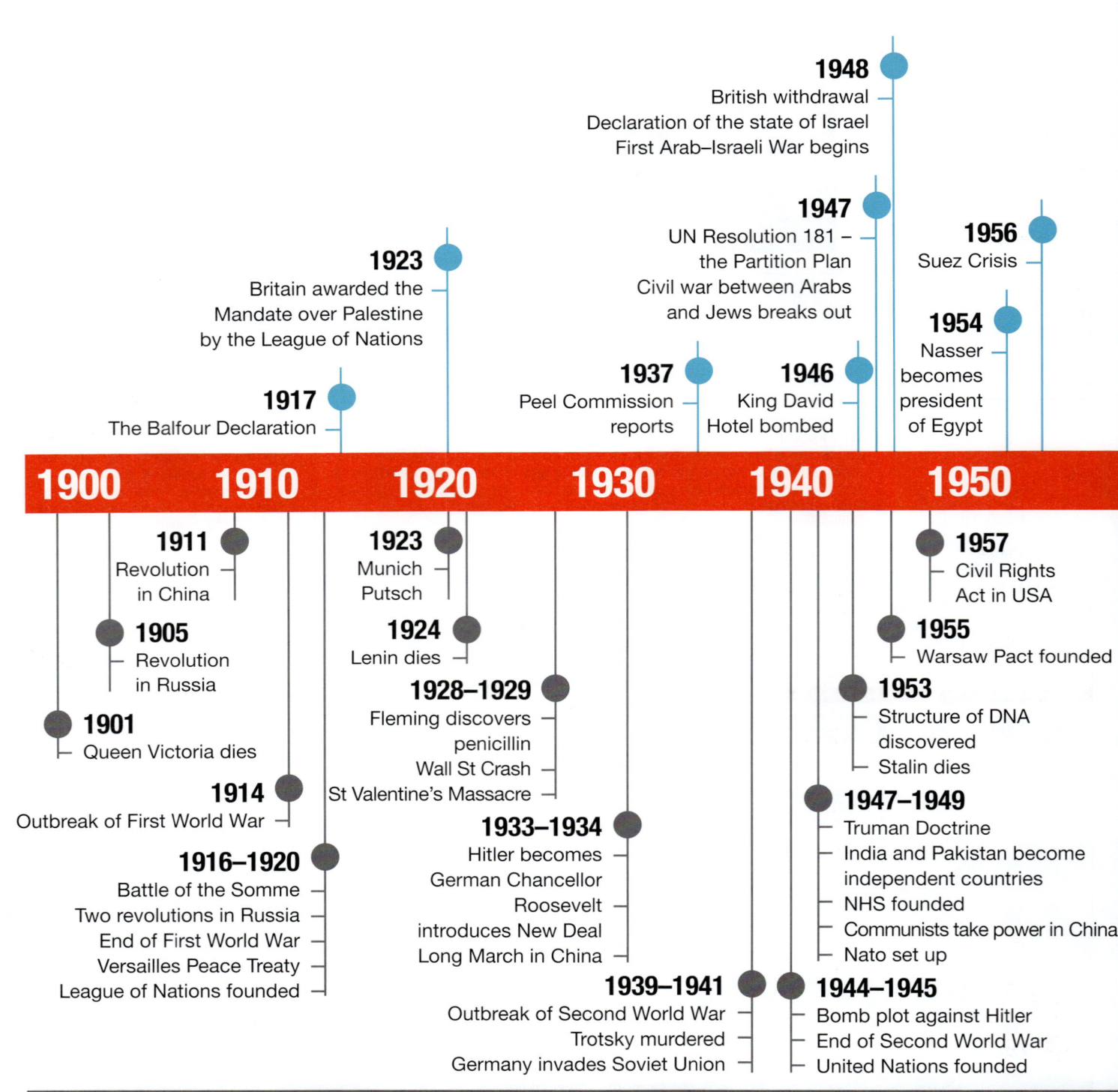

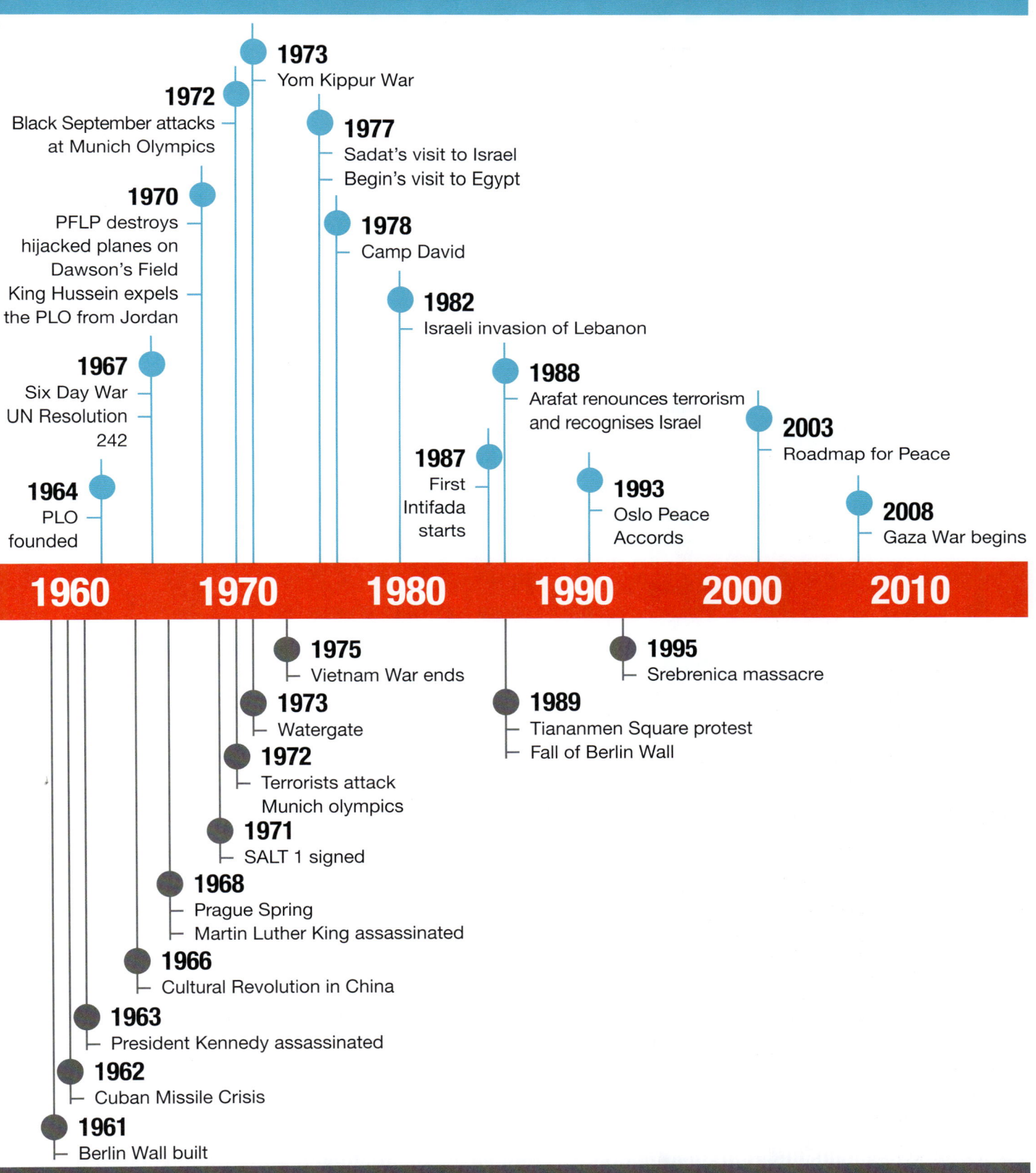

1. BUILD-UP OF TENSION IN PALESTINE, 1917–48

LEARNING OBJECTIVES

- Understand how Britain came to rule Palestine as a Mandate
- Understand the conflicting interests and demands of Arabs and Jews in the Mandate
- Understand the tactics used by Arabs and Jews against the British, and their impact.

In November 1917, the British foreign secretary Lord Arthur Balfour issued a very short – but extremely important – declaration saying that the British government sympathised with the idea of creating a home for Jews in Palestine, as long as the interests of Palestinian Arabs were not harmed. A month later, British soldiers occupied Jerusalem. They stayed for 30 years. Throughout that time, Britain attempted to carry out the ideas behind the Balfour Declaration. But as Jews migrated in unexpectedly high numbers to Palestine, tension with the outraged local Arab population led to clashes. To restore peace, Britain placed strict limits on Jewish immigration – but that in turn angered Jews, especially after the horrors of the Holocaust had been exposed. They began terrorist and publicity campaigns to force the British to leave. Exhausted, Britain handed the problem over to the United Nations.

In November 1947, the United Nations voted in favour of a very controversial plan: to partition Palestine into two states, one for Jews and one for Arabs. For many Jews, that UN vote was the realisation of a hard-fought campaign to establish a Jewish homeland, somewhere free from the persecution that Jews had suffered for centuries. However, for Palestinian Arabs, the UN vote was an insult. From their point of view, this was their land and the UN had no right to divide it. A vicious civil war between Palestinian Arabs and Jews immediately broke out.

1.1 BACKGROUND (NON-EXAMINABLE)

LEARNING OBJECTIVES

- Understand the background to events in the Middle East from 1917.

This section is to help you understand the problems that arose from 1917. It will not be assessed in the examination.

This book is about one of the tensest conflicts in the Middle East – the continuing dispute between Israelis and Palestinians. The dispute is over a small piece of land between the Mediterranean Sea and the River Jordan. One city in this land, Jerusalem, has deep religious significance for three world religions: Judaism, Christianity and Islam. Though the dispute between Israelis and Palestinians is about more than religious claims, issues about religion have played an important part in the conflict.

CLAIMS TO THE HOLY LAND

For Jews, the **Holy Land** is their **Promised Land**. Jews settled here over 3,000 years ago and, despite internal divisions, periods of exile and being conquered several times, Jews lived here until the 2nd century AD. According to Jewish tradition, in about 1000 BC the second Israelite king, David, captured the city of Jerusalem and made it his capital. His son, King Solomon, built a temple in Jerusalem to house the Ark of the Covenant, a sacred chest that contained the Ten Commandments that God had given to Moses.

In the 1st century BC, the Romans conquered this land, which they named Judea, or land of the Jews. Following a Jewish rebellion, the Romans destroyed the temple and banned Jews from living in Jerusalem. That did not stop the rebels. The Romans reacted harshly: many Jews were executed; others were sent across the Roman Empire as slaves or exiles. It is an event known as the **Diaspora**. The Romans then renamed the land Palestine and many non-Jews settled there.

Jerusalem is significant for Christians too. According to Christian tradition, it is where Jesus Christ celebrated his Last Supper, where he was **crucified** and where he rose from the dead. When the Roman Empire converted to Christianity in the 4th century AD, the Church of the Holy Sepulchre was built on the site of Jesus' crucifixion and tomb, and Jerusalem became the holiest site in Christendom.

Jerusalem and Palestine came under Muslim control in about 640 AD, when Arabs conquered the area and converted much of the population to Islam. The area remained in Muslim hands until 1917 (except for a 90-year gap of control by Christian **crusaders**, from 1099–1187). Control of Jerusalem was important to Muslims because it is the third holiest city in Islam. According to Islamic tradition, the Prophet Mohammed visited Jerusalem in 610 and ascended into heaven for one night. The Arabs built two important holy buildings in Jerusalem: the Al-Aqsa Mosque (built on the spot where Mohammed ascended into heaven) and the Dome of the Rock.

▲ Holy sites in the Old City of Jerusalem. The wall at the front is known as the 'Wailing Wall'. It is one of the holiest sites in Judaism. Above this wall Solomon's Temple once stood, possibly located where the golden-roofed Islamic Dome of the Rock now stands. (The Al-Aqsa Mosque is just out of sight to the right.)

KEY TERM

Diaspora movement of people away from their original homeland. In this case it refers to the Jewish Diaspora of the first and second centuries AD

BUILD-UP OF TENSION — THE MIDDLE EAST, 1917–2012

ANTI-SEMITISM

Despite the Diaspora, Jews never gave up hope of returning to Jerusalem. This hope became very important because, over the next 1,900 years, wherever they settled, the Jews were often treated very badly. They were victims of **anti-Semitism**. In some countries they were forced to wear special clothing, to pay extra taxes and to live in **ghettoes**. Sometimes they were victims of violent attacks. Some countries expelled Jews completely, as England did in 1290 and Spain in 1492.

To lessen the impact of anti-Semitism, some Jews tried to mix in with the local culture in the country where they had settled, by adopting the clothes and language. Some fought for equal rights. Others, especially in Eastern Europe and Russia, maintained their Jewish identity and culture. They ate different food (kosher), spoke different languages (Yiddish and Hebrew), and shared traditions that set them apart from others. This separation, they hoped, would protect them from anti-Semitic attacks.

But, if anything, anti-Semitism grew even worse in the late 19th century, especially in Russia. In 1881, Tsar Alexander II was assassinated by a group calling itself the People's Will. One of the group was Jewish, and perhaps because of this a new wave of anti-Semitic attacks shook Russia. Over the next 25 years, about 3 million Jews fled the violence in Russia.

> **EXTEND YOUR KNOWLEDGE**
>
> **THE DREYFUS AFFAIR**
>
> Anti-Semitism was also present in France. In 1894, a young Jewish French army captain called Alfred Dreyfus was accused of spying for the Germans. Though Dreyfus strongly protested his innocence, he was found guilty of treason and sentenced to life imprisonment. But first he had to endure a public humiliation: as drums rolled, he was publicly stripped of his army rank and then driven through Paris as huge crowds shouted 'death to the Jews'. It took his supporters 12 years to prove that Dreyfus was innocent and a victim of anti-Semitism. One of the journalists reporting on the Dreyfus affair was Theodor Herzl.

THE RISE OF ZIONISM

A Jewish journalist called Theodor Herzl became convinced that anti-Semitism would always exist; it could never be defeated. In 1896, he published a book explaining his view that the only solution for Jews was for them to have their own country. The best place for this would be the historic homeland of the Jews, Palestine. Herzl called his idea 'Zionism', because Zion was an alternative name for Jerusalem. The following year, he organised the first ever **Zionist** World Conference, to which 206 delegates came from 16 countries. Until he died in 1904, Herzl championed the idea of Palestine as a homeland for Jews.

However, if the Jews wanted to return to Palestine then they had to negotiate with the power that controlled it since 1516: the **Ottoman Empire**. The Ottoman authorities permitted some immigration and about 50,000 Jews had moved to Palestine by 1900. But the Ottomans were not prepared to do more because they did not want to risk more trouble from the Arabs who already lived there.

> **KEY TERM**
>
> **Ottoman Empire** also known as the Turkish Empire, the Ottoman Empire was founded in 1299 and lasted until 1918

> **ACTIVITY**
>
> Draw a timeline 15 cm long. Using the scale 0.5 cm = 100 years, mark off every 500 years from 1000 BC to 1900 AD.
> 1. Roughly mark off when Jerusalem was dominated by Jews, Muslims and Christians.
> 2. Add notes to your timeline explaining the religious importance of Jerusalem to each of these three faiths.
> 3. Indicate on your timeline when Jerusalem fell under the control of the Roman Empire, then Arabs, and then the Ottoman Empire.

ARAB NATIONALISM

Though the Ottomans were Muslim, they were Turkish, not Arabs. Arabs throughout the Middle East, including those living in Palestine, hated living under Ottoman control. They were treated harshly and forced to pay heavy taxes. When the teaching of Turkish in schools was made compulsory, many felt that Arabic culture was being insulted. Clashes between Turks and Arabs became frequent and violent. Though the Arabs were not united, demands for independence had become widespread by 1914.

1.2 THE BALFOUR DECLARATION, NOVEMBER 1917

LEARNING OBJECTIVES

- Understand the impact of the First World War on events in the Middle East
- Understand reasons for the Balfour Declaration
- Understand the significance of the Balfour Declaration.

EXTEND YOUR KNOWLEDGE

PALESTINIAN ARABS

It has been calculated from Ottoman records that about 660,000 Muslim Arabs and 80,000 Christian Arabs were living in Palestine in 1914. About one-third lived in larger towns, while two-thirds lived in villages and smaller towns. The phrase 'Palestinian Arabs' is used for this Arabic-speaking population, regardless of their religion.

KEY TERM

Suez Canal a canal in Egypt; it is 170 km long and links the Mediterranean to the Red Sea. It enables ships travelling between the east and the west to avoid a 2-week-long journey around Africa. By the 1950s, 15,000 ships and two-thirds of Europe's oil passed through it every year

SOURCE A

From a memorandum written by Lord Arthur Balfour in 1919.

In Palestine we do not propose even to go through the form of consulting the wishes of the present inhabitants of the country… Zionism, be it right or wrong, good or bad, is rooted in age-long traditions, in present needs, in future hopes, of far profounder import than the desires and prejudices of the 700,000 Arabs who now inhabit the land.

THE IMPACT OF THE FIRST WORLD WAR

Herzl's Zionist goal might have come to nothing had it not been for the First World War and British involvement in the Middle East. During the war, Britain made three contradictory agreements.

1. The first agreement, the McMahon-Hussein Agreement, was made in 1915 with the Arabs. They agreed to help the British defeat the Ottomans (who were allies of Germany) in return for support for Arab independence after the war. The Arabs carried out their part of the bargain and, by 1918 the entire Ottoman Empire had collapsed. Ten million Arabs had been freed from Turkish rule and most, including those living in Palestine, believed they had won their independence. They were unaware, though, that the British troops occupying Jerusalem intended to stay, and that the British government had signed two other agreements.

2. Britain's second agreement, the Sykes-Picot Agreement, was made with France in 1916. Anxious to protect their access to oil supplies in the Middle East and their control of the **Suez Canal**, both countries secretly arranged to divide up the Ottoman Empire between themselves after the war. Palestine would fall under international control. Arab hopes of independence were largely ignored.

3. Britain's final agreement concerned Palestine alone, and is known as the Balfour Declaration.

In November 1917, as British troops closed in on Jerusalem, the British Foreign Secretary Lord Arthur Balfour wrote a letter to Baron Rothschild, a leader of the British Jewish community. The Balfour Declaration, as it is called, said that the British government would look favourably upon Zionist plans to establish a home for Jews in Palestine, as long as this did not harm the rights of Arabs already living there.

Balfour's motives in sending the letter are unclear. Here are some possibilities.

- Perhaps Balfour was sympathetic to Zionist aims. He knew Lord Rothschild well and a political colleague, Herbert Samuel, was Jewish and a keen Zionist. Balfour also knew Chaim Weizmann, leader of the World Zionist movement, and had met with him before the war.
- More likely the Declaration was related to the war effort. Balfour hoped that American Zionists would put pressure on their government to send more troops to help on the Western Front, where casualties (injuries and deaths) were enormous. America had declared war on Germany 8 months earlier, but only 14,000 troops had arrived.
- Perhaps Balfour was also looking to the future: this was a way to win American support for Britain's plans in the Middle East after the war. Britain needed to secure its hold on all territory close to the Suez Canal, which was crucial for British trade with India.

One thing is certain: Balfour did not consider the views of the Arabs living in Palestine, as Source A makes clear.

SOURCE B

The Balfour Declaration, November 1917.

> Foreign Office,
> November 2nd, 1917.
>
> Dear Lord Rothschild,
>
> I have much pleasure in conveying to you, on behalf of His Majesty's Government, the following declaration of sympathy with Jewish Zionist aspirations which has been submitted to, and approved by, the Cabinet
>
> "His Majesty's Government view with favour the establishment in Palestine of a national home for the Jewish people, and will use their best endeavours to facilitate the achievement of this object, it being clearly understood that nothing shall be done which may prejudice the civil and religious rights of existing non-Jewish communities in Palestine, or the rights and political status enjoyed by Jews in any other country"
>
> I should be grateful if you would bring this declaration to the knowledge of the Zionist Federation.

1.3 THE BRITISH MANDATE TO 1945

LEARNING OBJECTIVES

- Understand the terms of Britain's Mandate
- Understand the reasons for Palestinian Arab unrest in the 1920s and 1930s
- Understand the solution proposed by the Peel Commission and how this was received by both Palestinian Arabs and Jews
- Understand the impact of the Second Word War on the Mandate.

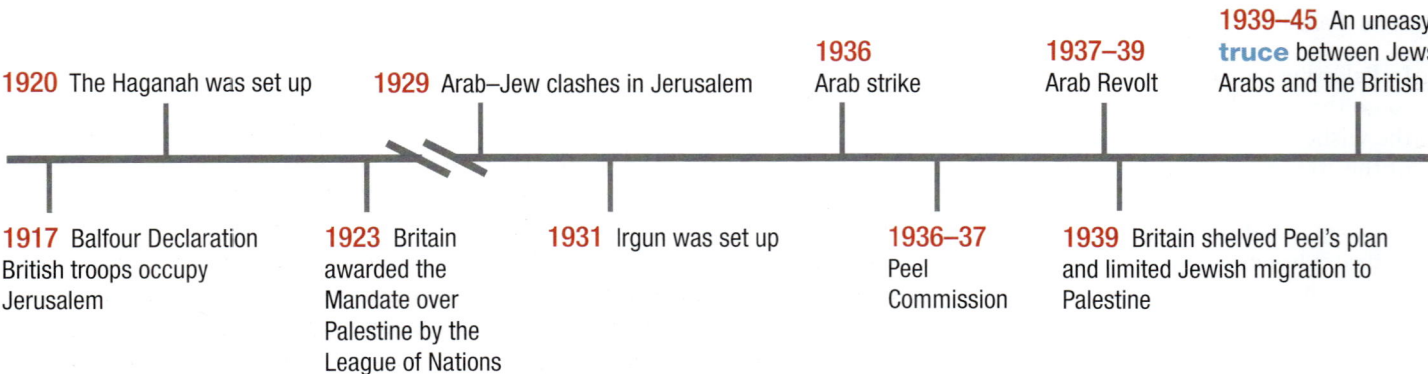

1920 The Haganah was set up
1929 Arab–Jew clashes in Jerusalem
1936 Arab strike
1937–39 Arab Revolt
1939–45 An uneasy truce between Jews, Arabs and the British

1917 Balfour Declaration British troops occupy Jerusalem
1923 Britain awarded the Mandate over Palestine by the League of Nations
1931 Irgun was set up
1936–37 Peel Commission
1939 Britain shelved Peel's plan and limited Jewish migration to Palestine

BUILD-UP OF TENSION
THE MIDDLE EAST, 1917–2012

KEY TERM

Mandate the official permission given to one of the League's members to govern a territory that had previously been ruled by Germany or Turkey. In this case, Britain was given the authority to rule Palestine, as long as certain conditions were met

EXTEND YOUR KNOWLEDGE

DAVID BEN-GURION

David Ben-Gurion was a passionate Zionist. In 1906, aged 20, he had migrated to Palestine from his home in Russian-controlled Poland. He became involved in politics, worked as a farmer and helped to defend Jewish settlements. In 1935, he was elected chairman of the Jewish Agency, which made him the main spokesman for the Jewish community in Palestine. After the Second World War, he led the struggle for independence and, in 1949, he became Israel's first prime minster.

▶ Figure 1.1 Palestine's changing population

In 1923, the League of Nations (the forerunner of the United Nations – see page 15) formally gave Britain the **Mandate** to rule over Palestine. Its terms were clear: Britain had to protect the rights of Palestinian Arabs, establish a homeland for Jews, and prepare the country for independence. It proved to be an impossible balancing act.

Palestinian Arabs were shocked and angered by the Mandate. They were furious that they had not been granted independence immediately. Nor had they been consulted about the use of Palestine, their land, as a Jewish homeland. It seemed they had just exchanged Ottoman rule for British.

For Jews, the Mandate enabled a Zionist dream to come true. Palestine would now be the homeland where Jews could be free from persecution.

Although there were only about 84,000 Jews in Palestine in 1922 (about 11 per cent of the total population), they were well organised about attracting new settlers.

The Jewish Agency was set up to encourage immigration to Palestine and to help new arrivals to buy land and organise schools. A defence force (the Haganah) was formed to protect new settlements. By 1931, Jewish numbers in Palestine had more than doubled to about 175,000 (about 17 per cent of the population). From 1933 to 1935, another 135,000 arrived. They were mostly German Jews fleeing **Nazism** and Hitler's anti-Semitic policies. By 1936, more than a quarter of Palestine's population was Jewish.

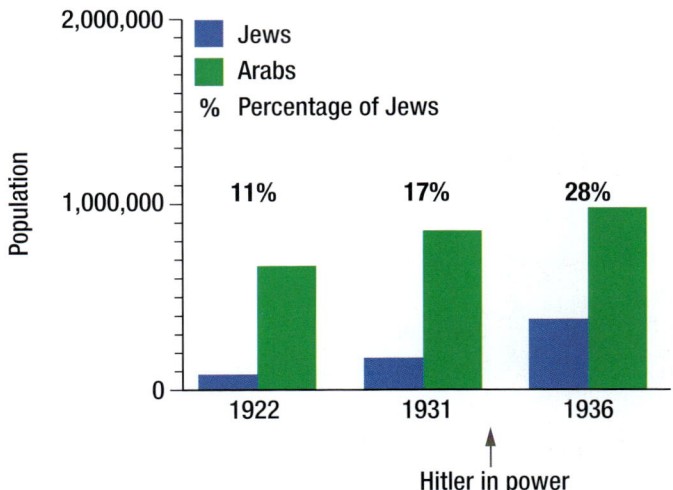

CLASHES BETWEEN JEWS AND PALESTINIANS

Palestinian Arabs objected strongly to Britain appearing to be favouring Jews. They had been cheated out of independence to start with and now they felt threatened by the scale of Jewish immigration and Jewish land purchases.

As the Jewish population grew, tension between them and the Arabs increased. Tension soon turned into violence. Clashes between two rival Jewish political parties on May Day in 1921 led to a rumour that Jews were attacking Arabs. This angered Palestinian Arabs in the city of Jaffa, who attacked local Jews and Jewish property, leaving 47 Jews and 48 Arabs dead. In August 1929, angry clashes occurred over holy sites in Jerusalem.

These grew into 4 days of bloody **riots** and mob violence throughout Palestine, leaving 133 Jews and 116 Arabs dead. Some Jews were angry that the British had not provided enough protection: one group formed Irgun, a terrorist organisation dedicated to forming a Jewish state by violence if necessary.

THE ARAB STRIKE, 1936

Seven years later, a full-blown Arab protest began. Encouraged by the fact that Syrian and Iraqi Arabs had won political rights by going on general strike, Palestinian Arabs decided to use the same tactic. They demanded an end to Jewish immigration, an end to land sales and a national government of their own. Until those conditions were met, they refused to work or to pay taxes, and **boycotted** all trade with the British. At the same time, roads, railways and oil pipes, and British troops, were attacked.

EXTEND YOUR KNOWLEDGE

JAFFA ORANGES

The orange orchards of Palestine employed over 100,000 workers in the 1930s. The variety grown was called the Jaffa orange, after the ancient port of Jaffa, and was famed for its sweetness. The Jaffa Cake, a new biscuit invented in 1927, was named after the orange.

The British reaction to the strike was harsh: Palestinian leaders were arrested, rebels were flogged and suspect villages were searched for weapons. For 6 months, 20,000 British troops struggled to control the situation. Then, in October 1936, at Britain's request, neighbouring Arab states got involved and called for calm. Palestinian Arabs agreed to end the strike (perhaps because they needed time to collect in the orange harvest).

THE PEEL COMMISSION, 1936–37

The level of Arab discontent alarmed the British government. It set up a commission to investigate the causes of unrest in Palestine and to propose a solution. Led by William Peel, the commission investigated the situation for 6 months. Over 100 witnesses were questioned. In July 1937, Lord Peel published his 400-page report. He said that the Mandate could never succeed. There was no common ground at all between the Arab and Jewish communities. They differed in religion, culture, dress, language and – above all – in their plans for Palestine's future. The situation had reached a **deadlock**. Peel said the only solution was to end the Mandate and **partition** the country between the two communities. Only a small part would remain under British control. In the meantime, he recommended that all Jewish immigration to what would be Arab territory should stop.

ACTIVITY

Why do you think Peel suggested that one part of Palestine remain under British control? Hint: it contained Jerusalem and Bethlehem.

EXTEND YOUR KNOWLEDGE

PEEL

Lord Peel's grandfather was Sir Robert Peel, the man who founded London's police force. Two terms for policemen – 'peelers' and 'bobbies' – come from Sir Robert's name.

▲ Figure 1.2 Map showing Peel's partition proposal in 1937

BUILD-UP OF TENSION — THE MIDDLE EAST, 1917–2012

REACTIONS TO PEEL'S PROPOSAL

Though they disliked the details of the plan, most Jews accepted the idea of partition. It was better than nothing, in the view of David Ben-Gurion. However, Palestinian Arabs rejected the Peel Partition Scheme completely. From their point of view, giving any land at all to Jews was unjust. Almost 300,000 Arabs would have to live in the Jewish state (unless they were moved to the proposed Arab state, something Peel favoured). Furthermore, the scheme would mean the most fertile land – including 90 per cent of the orange groves – being in Jewish hands.

THE ARAB REVOLT 1937–39

SOURCE C
British troops try to control a riot in Jerusalem during the Arab Revolt.

Palestinian Arabs reacted angrily to Peel's recommendations. This time, their revolt involved increasingly violent attacks against British forces and Jews.

Helped by 15,000 men from the Haganah, 50,000 British troops used harsh tactics. Rebel houses were destroyed, **curfews** were put in place, and thousands of Arabs were arrested and held without trial. Many were beaten or tortured. Villages suspected of helping rebels were occupied and their inhabitants expelled. Weapons were confiscated. To prevent **sniper** attacks, British soldiers tied Arab hostages to the bonnets of their lorries. In Source D, a British soldier recalls what might happen to the hostage at the end of the journey.

ACTIVITY

Working with a partner:
1 What do you think Source D tells us about British attitudes to Palestinian Arabs?
2 Would Balfour have agreed with this view? Read Source B to help you.

SOURCE D
From an account given by Arthur Lane, a British private serving in Palestine in 1937.

The driver would switch his wheel back and to, to make the truck waver and the poor native on the front would roll off onto the deck. Well, if he was lucky, he'd get away with a broken leg but if he was unlucky the truck coming up behind would hit him. But nobody bothered to pick up the pieces; they were left. You know, we were there, we were the masters, we were the bosses and whatever we did was right.

EXTEND YOUR KNOWLEDGE

MASSACRE AT AL-BASSA, 1938
A particularly brutal massacre of Palestinian Arabs took place at al-Bassa, a village with a mixed Christian and Muslim population in the far north of Palestine. On 6 September 1938, four British soldiers were killed when their armoured car ran over a land mine. In retaliation, British troops sprayed the village with machine gun fire for 20 minutes and then burned it down. About 20 Arabs were rounded up. Some tried to run away and were shot; the remainder were put on a bus, which was forced over a land mine laid by the soldiers. It destroyed the bus and killed all those in it. The other villagers were then forced to dig a pit and throw in all the bodies.

By 1939, when the revolt ended, about 250 British troops and 300 Jews had been killed. On the Palestinian Arab side, about 5,000 had been killed while 15,000 had been wounded. In fact, over ten per cent of the adult male Arab population had been killed, wounded, imprisoned or exiled. Among the exiles were all the leaders of the Palestinian Arabs. In addition, the British had confiscated their weapons. It left the Palestinian side in a particularly weak position.

BUILD-UP OF TENSION — THE MIDDLE EAST, 1917–2012

EXAM-STYLE QUESTION

A01 A02

SKILLS ADAPTIVE LEARNING

Explain **two** causes of Arab unrest in Palestine in the 1920s and 1930s.

(8 marks)

HINT
This question is asking about causation. You need to read the chapter carefully and find two reasons why Palestinian Arabs protested in this period. You need to explain each reason, and provide one or two pieces of supporting evidence.

PALESTINE AND THE SECOND WORLD WAR

The threat of war with Germany led to a sudden change in British policy in Palestine in early 1939. For the British to win a war, oil would be needed from the Middle East and this would require Arab co-operation. The Peel Plan was shelved and the suppression stopped. The British also limited the number of Jewish immigrants allowed into Palestine to 10,000 a year for 5 years.

The timing of this decision could not have been worse for European Jews, who were desperate to escape Nazi persecution. Palestinian Jews protested on the streets. Nevertheless, when war did break out, most agreed that a truce with Britain was necessary until the Nazis had been defeated. Along with some 25,000 Arabs, about 27,000 Jews from the Haganah and Irgun fought with British forces during the war. But a few members of Irgun disagreed with this policy: they set up the extremist group Lehi and continued the struggle against Britain.

THE HOLOCAUST

On 15 April 1945, as the Second World War was drawing to a close, British troops liberated Bergen Belsen, a Nazi concentration camp. The troops found 60,000 prisoners inside the camp, most seriously ill from typhus and chronic malnutrition. A further 13,000 dead bodies lay around.

ACTIVITY

It would be a good idea to start your own glossary. Write a short definition for each of the following words: anti-Semitism; Zionism; Mandate; Holocaust; Haganah; Irgun; Lehi.

As Allied troops liberated more camps, the full horrors of the Holocaust were uncovered. Six million Jewish men, women and children had been murdered. Survivors spoke of the appalling brutalities they had suffered – of hard labour, starvation, torture, humiliation, beatings, medical experiments and forced marches. Most had lost their entire families and their homes. For these survivors there was no reason to stay in Europe. Many wanted a new beginning, in the USA or in a state of their own, in Palestine. Shocking reports about the Holocaust meant there was a great deal of international sympathy to help them.

SOURCE E
A survivor of Bergen Belsen Camp, April 1945.

1.4 THE BRITISH MANDATE, 1945–47

LEARNING OBJECTIVES

- Understand the causes of the Jewish insurgency against the British, and the tactics used by both sides
- Understand the impact of the Jewish insurgency on Britain and on world opinion
- Understand the terms and impact of the United Nations' Partition Plan.

May 1945 End of the Second World War in Europe. Britain decides to allow only 1,500 Jews a month into Palestine

April 1946 Britain refuses to allow 100,000 Jewish refugees into Palestine

February 1947 Britain asks the UN to find a solution to the problems in Palestine

April 1945 British forces liberate Bergen Belsen

October 1945 Start of the Jewish insurgency

July 1946 Irgun blow up the King David Hotel in Jerusalem

July 1947 The SS *Exodus* is turned back from Palestine

The Holocaust had shown that the need for a Jewish homeland was greater than ever. At a Conference held in London in 1945, Zionists demanded the immediate creation of a Jewish state in Palestine. They hoped the British government would be sympathetic and help Holocaust survivors move to Palestine.

The Labour government elected in Britain in July 1945 had to tackle the Palestine issue immediately. Although there were about 250,000 Jews in 'displaced persons' camps in Europe, the problem of balancing the conflicting demands of Jews and Arabs remained. So the new British foreign secretary, Ernest Bevin, set a strict limit of 1,500 Jewish immigrants a month into Palestine. He had two main reasons:

- He believed that a flood of Jewish immigrants into Palestine would result in civil war between Arabs and Jews.
- Britain needed to keep on good terms with Arab states in the Middle East: the war had shown the importance of oil and Arab states like Saudi Arabia had huge reserves of it. These Arab states did not support Jewish migration to Palestine.

THE JEWISH INSURGENCY IN PALESTINE, 1945–47

Angered by Britain's attitude, Zionist organisations in Palestine abandoned the truce that most had adopted during the war.

▼ EXTREMIST GROUPS LIKE THE IRGUN AND LEHI AIMED TO:

- wage a campaign of violence against the British to force them to remove their troops from Palestine.
- horrify the British public into demanding a British withdrawal from Palestine.

▼ MODERATE GROUPS LIKE THE HAGANAH AIMED TO:

- help as many Holocaust survivors as possible to reach Palestine by whatever means necessary.
- get worldwide sympathy for the establishment of a Jewish state.

In October 1945, both extremist and moderate groups worked together: they blew up the Palestine railway system in 153 places to hamper British communications. Irgun and Lehi then led the campaign of violence. Over the next 24 months, they targeted anything that was British. They blew up offices, attacked police stations, **sabotaged** oil pipes, bombed airfields and bridges, placed land mines on roads, and destroyed radio stations and telephone lines. They stole British weapons and robbed banks to gain money. Seventy three British troops were killed in 1946 alone. Other acts were designed to destroy British morale. In December 1946, two Irgun terrorists were sentenced to 18 years' imprisonment and 18 strokes of the cane; in **retaliation**, Menachem Begin, the leader of Irgun, had four British soldiers kidnapped and beaten with 18 strokes each.

THE BOMBING OF THE KING DAVID HOTEL

The single deadliest act of anti-British terror committed by the Irgun was the bombing of the luxurious King David Hotel in Jerusalem, which contained the headquarters of both the Mandate administration and the British Army in its southern wing. Security was tight, except in the basement. On 22 July 1946, just before noon, a lorry drove up to the tradesmen's entrance of the

SOURCE F

British soldiers dig their way through the ruins in search of survivors at the King David Hotel in Jerusalem.

BUILD-UP OF TENSION — THE MIDDLE EAST, 1917–2012

EXTEND YOUR KNOWLEDGE

OPERATION AGATHA

In June 1946, the British authorities launched a massive operation against the Zionist underground organisations that they blamed for all the chaos in Palestine. Over 10,000 British security forces raided buildings, confiscated weapons and papers, and arrested 2,700 Jewish suspects. The bombing of the King David Hotel was Irgun's revenge for this operation. The Irgun had another purpose: they believed that this was where all the confiscated papers were.

hotel. In it were Irgun members disguised as Arabs, who then entered the building and placed milk churns containing explosives by the main columns supporting the southern wing. The bombs were timed to go off at 12.37 p.m. Menachem Begin later said that three warnings were telephoned through. If so, the warnings never reached the right people. The building was not evacuated and the explosion destroyed much of the southern wing, killing 91 people, including 41 Arabs, 28 Britons and 17 Jews. Most were civilians.

The bombing of the King David Hotel had significant consequences. It caused **outrage**. The Haganah publicly criticised the Irgun and the British announced a high state of alert. Palestinian Jews were subject to increasingly harsh restrictions, including random searches, military curfews, road blocks and mass arrests. However, government policy on Jewish immigration to Palestine remained unchanged.

THE IMPACT OF JEWISH TERRORISM ON BRITAIN

Terrorism like the King David Hotel bombing did not immediately change government policy, but it did have an impact. It made the Mandate increasingly expensive to run, yet it was hard to justify keeping 100,000 troops in Palestine when Britain was still recovering from the Second World War. It also began to turn opinion in Britain against the Mandate. As far as the public were concerned, the war with Germany was over, and they did not understand why British soldiers were still dying. The troops on the ground were also increasingly demoralised (see Source G).

EXTEND YOUR KNOWLEDGE

CYPRUS

Cyprus was part of the British Empire. The British established 12 camps on the island to inter (hold) Jewish refugees who were attempting to get to Palestine despite the British limit of 1,500 immigrants a month. Eventually, over 50,000 refugees were kept in these camps.

SOURCE G

A British Private in Palestine in 1946–47 recalls how Zionist terrorism had an impact even on his leisure time.

We carried our rifles at all times. We never went out with less than four people. If we sat in a café, two or three men kept watch while the others drank their beer. When we went to the beach to swim it had to be in a party of thirty. It was depressing. It was boring, hot, we had no letters and there was a feeling that there was no reason for us being where we were. I had my metal cigarette case engraved with a Star of David. I thought it might help me if I were kidnapped by the Irgun or Stern Gang [Lehi].

THE SS EXODUS

While Irgun and Lehi conducted their campaign of terror, the Haganah and the Jewish Agency smuggled Jews into Palestine. They acquired ships, filled them with would-be immigrants and then tried to break through the British **blockade**. On one level, the campaign was a failure: very few vessels got through. But, in terms of publicity for the Zionist cause, it was a huge success. Every time the Royal Navy turned a ship away, or put refugees into camps on Cyprus, Britain's reputation was damaged and sympathy for the Jewish cause was increased.

KEY TERM

blockade when a place is closed off to prevent goods or people from entering or leaving

In July 1947, for example, the Haganah bought an old American passenger ship, renamed it *Exodus 1947*, and sailed it to France. There it picked up 4,500 Jews, many of them Holocaust survivors. The *Exodus* then sailed for Palestine, where it was stopped by the Royal Navy and the passengers were transported back to France. When the passengers refused to leave the ship and went on hunger strike, the British took them to Hamburg in Germany, where they were forced to return to refugee camps. The incident caused worldwide outrage against Britain, and played a major part in moving sympathy towards the idea of establishing a Jewish state.

SOURCE H

The SS *Exodus* being refused permission to dock at Haifa by British authorities, July 1947.

EXAM-STYLE QUESTION

A01   A02

SKILLS   ADAPTIVE LEARNING

Explain **two** causes of the Jewish insurgency in Palestine in the years 1945 to 1947.

(8 marks)

HINT

This question is testing your ability to explain why an event happened. A good answer would include supporting details. Read page 10 again to help you and remember to write about two causes.

US SUPPORT FOR ZIONISM

Holocaust survivors' demands for a Jewish state in Palestine met with much sympathy in the USA, which had over 5 million Jews in 1945. Some volunteers helped to smuggle immigrants into Palestine. Others supported Zionism with money: in 1945 alone, Americans gave over $46 million to the Zionist cause. Meanwhile, the US press printed articles that encouraged Jewish terrorism (see Source I).

> **SOURCE I**
>
> From an article in the New York Herald Tribune, 15 May 1947, written by Ben Hecht, a Hollywood script writer.
>
> The Jews of America are with you. You are their champion. You are the grin that they wear. You are the feather in their hats. Every time you blow up a British arsenal, or wreck a British jail, or send a British rail-road sky high, or rob a British bank, or let go with your guns and bombs at the British betrayers and invaders of your homeland, the Jews of America make a little holiday in their hearts.

US Zionists put pressure on President Harry Truman to help Holocaust survivors and, since he was deeply sympathetic to them, Truman agreed. The USA admitted 150,000 Jewish refugees immediately after the war. Truman also repeatedly asked Britain to allow into Palestine 100,000 Jews still living in European refugee camps. When Ernest Bevin refused, arguing that it would cause an Arab revolt, the USA applied economic pressure. Britain could not afford to offend the USA since it relied on US aid for its post-war recovery. A wish to avoid a clash with the USA was an important reason why Britain eventually gave up the Mandate.

BRITAIN HANDS OVER THE PROBLEM

By early 1947, it was clear that the British position in Palestine was impossible. It could not agree to Zionist demands to allow in Jewish refugees without angering Arabs. It could not stop Jewish terrorism. It lacked money. Worn out by negative publicity, US pressure, and demands from the British public to end the situation, the British government decided to ask the newly formed **United Nations** to come up with a solution to the Palestinian problem.

> **KEY TERM**
>
> United Nations an international organisation made up of most of the countries of the world. It was founded in 1945 to promote peace and security, and has its headquarters in New York

> **ACTIVITY**
>
> 1 Draw a spider diagram showing all the reasons why the British position in Palestine had become impossible by 1947.
> 2 Are any of your reasons connected? Draw a line between them and explain the link.
> 3 Which reasons were the most significant? Pick two and write a paragraph explaining your choice.

1.5 UNITED NATIONS INVOLVEMENT IN PALESTINE

LEARNING OBJECTIVES

- Understand the United Nations Partition Plan and reactions to it
- Understand the importance of UN Resolution 181
- Understand the significance of the civil war in Palestine.

May 1947 The UN sets up UNSCOP

September 1947 UNSCOP proposes the Partition Plan

Dec 1947–May 1948 Palestine descends into civil war

February 1947 The British ask the UN to come up with a solution

June–August 1947 UNSCOP tours Palestine

November 1947 The UN votes in favour of the Partition Plan (UN Resolution 181)

May 1948 Israel created; the British leave

In May 1947, the United Nations set up a Special Committee on Palestine (UNSCOP) to investigate possible solutions to the problem. The UNSCOP delegates came from 11 different nations, representing every continent. That summer, the delegates toured Palestine. They gathered evidence and met British representatives and Jewish leaders. They visited Jewish settlements, where they were warmly welcomed. They talked with Jewish refugees in British detention camps, and some witnessed what happened to the Holocaust survivors on board the SS *Exodus*. However, it proved more difficult to get Arab views. Arabs boycotted UNSCOP: they said it was pro-Zionist and had no right to be there. The delegates faced hostility or were ignored in Arab areas, although they did meet privately with an ex-Muslim mayor of Jerusalem, and they travelled to Lebanon and Transjordan to gather the views of neighbouring Arab states.

THE UN PARTITION PLAN

In September 1947, UNSCOP reported back. By a majority decision, it recommended the partition of Palestine into separate Jewish and Arab states. Each state would be in three separate parts that were linked together. The two new states would have economic unity, with a shared currency and railways, roads, postal, telephone and telegraphic services all run for the common good. Jerusalem and Bethlehem would be under international control, since both had holy places that were sacred to Christians, Jews and Muslims.

▼ Population data from the report of UNSCOP, 1947

TERRITORY	ARAB AND OTHER POPULATION	% ARAB AND OTHER	JEWISH POPULATION	% JEWISH
Arab State	725,000	99%	10,000	1%
Jewish State	407,000	45%	498,000	55%
Jerusalem and the UN zone	105,000	51%	100,000	49%
Total	1,237,000	67%	608,000	33%

| BUILD-UP OF TENSION | THE MIDDLE EAST, 1917–2012 | 17 |

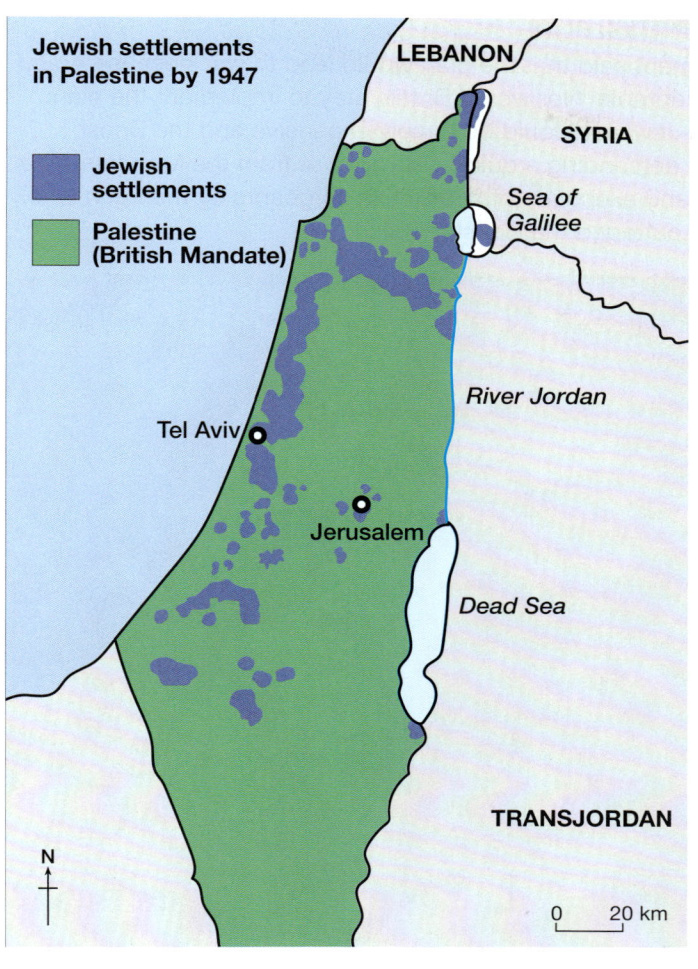

▲ Figure 1.3 A map showing Jewish settlements in 1947

▲ Figure 1.4 A map showing the Partition Plan

ACTIVITY

1. Look at Figure 1.4, which shows a map of the Partition Plan: write down your first impressions. For example, do you think splitting the territory in this way would work?
2. Look at Figure 1.3, Figure 1.4 and the table: why do you think the Arabs argued that the plan was unfair? Give some examples to support your points.
3. Was UNSCOP right to propose partition? Write one paragraph arguing in favour of the Partition Plan and one paragraph arguing against it.

EXTEND YOUR KNOWLEDGE

THE 'SERGEANTS AFFAIR', JULY 1947

One episode of Zionist terrorism more than any other caused outrage in Britain, and may have contributed to Britain's decision just to pull out. Two months before the Partition Plan was published, in July 1947, the Irgun kidnapped and hanged two British sergeants, as a reprisal for the execution of two Irgun members. The bodies of the sergeants were then hung up in an olive grove and booby trapped, injuring those who came to cut them down. The *Times* newspaper compared the Irgun to the Nazis, and there were anti-Semitic riots in Manchester, Liverpool, Glasgow and London. In Derby, a synagogue was burned down.

REACTIONS TO THE PARTITION PLAN

- The British government said that the plan would lead to war because Arabs would find it unacceptable. Nor would Britain stay to implement the plan: refereeing an Arab–Jew war would be hugely expensive and the British public were angrily demanding a quick **withdrawal** from the Mandate. The recent kidnapping and execution of two British sergeants by the Irgun (see Source J) had also outraged the British public.

SOURCE J

This image of two dead British sergeants was printed on the front page of the *Daily Express*.

- Arabs completely rejected the plan. From their point of view, the UN had no right to take away land against the wishes of its inhabitants. They complained that the Palestinians were being made to pay for the Holocaust. Nor was the Plan even fair. It gave over half of Palestine to the proposed Jewish state, despite the fact that Jews formed only one-third of the population. Jews only owned about seven per cent of the land, but they had also been given the most fertile parts of Palestine, in the north and on the coast.
- Most Jews accepted the plan, reluctantly. They had wanted Jerusalem to be their capital, but the plan would make even visiting the city difficult since it would be located deep within Arab territory. Furthermore, over 400,000 Arabs would be living in the proposed Jewish state, where Arabs would own 80 per cent of the land. The land given to the Jewish state in the south was a desert, called the Negev. Nevertheless, many felt the plan at least recognised the right of Jews to an independent state. However, for extremist Jews the plan was unacceptable. They insisted that Jerusalem had to be part of the new state.

BUILD-UP OF TENSION   THE MIDDLE EAST, 1917–2012

UN RESOLUTION 181

In November 1947, the Partition Plan was put to the vote in the full General Assembly of the United Nations. To be accepted, a two-thirds majority was needed. The USA knew that most western European states would vote in favour. The horrors of the Holocaust meant that there was a lot of sympathy for a Jewish homeland. Many European states would also follow the US lead because they were struggling to rebuild after the Second World War and needed financial support from the USA. However, still more votes in favour were needed, so the USA also put pressure on smaller states.

KEY TERMS

USSR Union of Soviet Socialist Republics. Sometimes called the Soviet Union, or incorrectly, Russia

Cold War the political tension and military rivalry that existed between the USA and the USSR between 1945 and 1991. Each saw the other as a threat to its continued survival. The war was 'cold' because it stopped short of a full-scale war between these two states, though each backed opposite sides in other conflicts like the Korean War

SOURCE K

An excerpt from a book written in 1978 by a British journalist working in the Middle East. He is explaining the pressure the USA put on other member nations of the UN to vote in favour of Resolution 181.

President Truman warned one of his secretaries that he would demand a full explanation if nations which normally lined up with the United States failed to do so on Palestine. Governments were swayed by the most unorthodox arguments. The Firestone Tyre and Rubber Company, with plantations in Liberia, brought pressure to bear on the Liberian Government. It was hinted to Latin American delegates that their vote for partition would greatly increase their chances of a Pan-American road project.

Equally crucial was the decision of the **USSR** to vote in favour of partition, since the USSR was able to put pressure on many Eastern European countries. The USSR hoped that the new Jewish state would be an ally in the **Cold War** that was then developing between itself and the USA. It thought this because many Jewish organisations in the Mandate were left-wing. The Irgun and Lehi were left-wing and the communal farming methods used in many Jewish settlements seemed similar to those used in the USSR.

The vote was taken on 29 November 1947. The vote in favour of partition was clear: 33 nations voted for, 13 against and ten **abstained**. UN Resolution 181 passed, which meant that the British would end their Mandate and the Partition Plan would be put into action by August 1948. The decision was met with joy by most Jews, but with anger and despair by Arabs.

EXAM-STYLE QUESTION

A01   **A02**

Explain **two** ways in which the UN Partition Plan (1947) was similar to the recommendations made by the Peel Commission (1937).   **(6 marks)**

HINT

This question is asking about similarities. You could look at the fact that both recommended the partition of Palestine, and both recommended that Jerusalem was given special status.

THE CIVIL WAR IN PALESTINE, DECEMBER 1947–MAY 1948

In December 1947, the British announced that they would be withdrawing from Palestine on 15 May 1948. For the next 5 months, Britain stood aside as Palestine descended into violent chaos. At first, Jewish forces were fighting just to hold on to the land that had been given to them by the UN. In the 12 days after the UN vote alone, angry Arab attacks on Jews left 79 dead. Jewish **reprisals** then meant further bloodshed. Riots descended into murderous attacks and many were killed on both sides. By February 1948, about 100,000 wealthier Palestinians had left the country to escape the violence. Their departure had a double impact: it deprived the Palestinian cause of leadership and it demoralised those who stayed.

PLAN D

In March 1948, the Haganah introduced Plan Dalet, or Plan D. This is much debated by historians. Some think it was a purely defensive plan that aimed to secure the future of Israel. This meant taking control of all the Arab towns and villages inside or close to the proposed Jewish territory. Their inhabitants would be under military control but, if they resisted, they were to be expelled. Even if it was not the intention, one modern Israeli historian has written that Plan D 'paved the way for the **ethnic cleansing** operation in Palestine' that followed, as villages were cleared of their Arab populations. Others think Plan D was an **offensive** plan: before the Mandate ended, the aim was to take control of all territory containing Jewish settlements, even if that territory would have been in the proposed Arab state.

> **KEY TERM**
>
> **ethnic cleansing** the action of forcing people to leave an area or country because of their racial or national group. This involves expelling them, or even sometimes killing them

DEIR YASSIN

If Plan D was offensive, then it helps to explain the emphasis put on making sure there was access to Jerusalem, where 100,000 Jews lived. They were virtually **besieged**. Arab forces controlled all access to the city, preventing food, water and medical supplies getting through. The fierce fighting to control the main road to Jerusalem saw one of the worst **atrocities** of the war.

The quiet Arab village of Deir Yassin lay high on a hill above this road. It had signed an agreement not to fight with its Jewish neighbours. On 9 April 1948, 100 Irgun and Lehi fighters massacred between 100–120 of its inhabitants (the exact number is debated), including many women and children. Menachem Begin led the attack and claimed that the action was justified on military grounds as Arab fighters were using Deir Yassin as a base.

Hoping to rally all Arabs into revenge, Arab radio stations quickly broadcast details of the atrocity. Arab fighters responded by ambushing a group of lorries containing Jewish nurses and doctors, killing 70. However, the broadcasts also had an unintended effect: panic-stricken that the same fate awaited them as the inhabitants of Deir Yassin, some 250,000 Palestinians abandoned their villages and towns, and fled to Arab-controlled territory for safety.

SOURCE L

A protest in Canada in 1967 about Deir Yassin.

BUILD-UP OF TENSION — THE MIDDLE EAST, 1917–2012

RECAP

RECALL QUIZ

1. What do the following words mean: anti-Semitism, Zionism, Mandate?
2. Who were the following: Arthur Balfour, William Peel, David Ben-Gurion, Menachem Begin?
3. Give two reasons why Balfour might have issued his Declaration.
4. What were the terms of Britain's Mandate over Palestine?
5. What proportion of Palestine's population were Jewish in 1922? And in 1936?
6. In what year did each of the following happen: the Balfour Declaration, the start of the Arab Revolt, the Peel Commission, the bombing of the King David Hotel, UN Resolution 181, the Deir Yassin massacre?
7. What demands did Palestinian Arabs make during the Arab Revolt?
8. Give two reasons why Palestinian Arabs rejected Peel's proposals and the UN Partition Plan.
9. What were the Jewish Agency, Haganah, Irgun, Lehi? Which was responsible for the bombing of the King David Hotel?
10. What were the UN, UNSCOP, UN Resolution 181?

CHECKPOINT

STRENGTHEN

S1 Explain the importance of the Balfour Declaration to Jews.
S2 Explain the importance of Peel's partition proposal to Palestinian Arabs.
S3 Explain the importance of the bombing of the King David Hotel to Britain.

CHALLENGE

C1 To help you to remember what happened, write a paragraph covering the period 1917–47 from the point of view of a Palestinian Arab.
C2 Now do the same again, but from the point of view of a Jewish immigrant to Palestine.
C3 Then do the same again, but from the point of view of a British soldier serving in Palestine.

SUMMARY

- In 1917, Britain issued the Balfour Declaration.
- The League of Nations gave Britain a Mandate to rule over Palestine.
- Jewish immigration to Palestine resulted in mounting tension between Arabs and Jews.
- In 1936, Palestinian Arabs went on general strike.
- The Peel Commission was appointed to investigate the causes of Arab unrest.
- Peel recommended an end to the Mandate and the partition of Palestine.
- Peel's plan was abandoned because of approaching war with Germany. Strict limits placed on Jewish immigration to Palestine.
- After the Second World War, Jewish forces launched terrorist and publicity campaigns to force Britain to create a Jewish state.
- The British asked the UN to come up with a solution to the Palestinian issue.
- In November 1947, the UN voted for partition (Resolution 181).
- Britain announced its departure, and Palestine fell into civil war.

EXAM GUIDANCE: PART (B) QUESTIONS

A01 A02

SKILLS ADAPTIVE LEARNING

Question to be answered: Explain two causes of the clashes between Palestinian Arabs and the British in the 1920s and 1930s. (8 marks)

1 Analysis Question 1: What is the question type testing?
In this question you have to demonstrate that you have knowledge and understanding of the key features and characteristics of the period studied. In this particular case it is knowledge and understanding of clashes between the Palestinian Arabs and the British.

You also have to explain and analyse historical events and periods to explain why something happened.

2 Analysis Question 2: What do I have to do to answer the question well?
Obviously you have to write about the clashes. But it isn't just a case of writing everything you know. You have to write about why they happened. To do this well, you need to give the detail showing what caused the clashes to happen, but you need to make sure you are explaining why that detail actually led to clashes. We call this explaining why your chosen causes produced the given result (in other words, the clashes).

In this case, there are many causes of the clashes. You might write about the distrust of the British or the immediate events leading to the clashes, for example.

3 Analysis Question 3: Are there any techniques I can use to make it very clear that I am doing what is needed to be successful?
This is an 8-mark question and you need to make sure you leave enough time to answer the other two questions fully (they are worth 22 marks in total). Therefore, you need to get straight into writing your answer. The question asks for two causes, so it's a good idea to write two paragraphs and to begin each paragraph with phrases like 'One cause was... ', 'Another cause was... '. You will get a maximum of 4 marks for each cause you explain, so make sure you do two causes.

How many marks you score for each cause will depend on how well you use accurate and factual information to explain why the clashes occurred.

BUILD-UP OF TENSION — THE MIDDLE EAST, 1917–2012

Answer A
Palestinian Arabs thought the British were favouring the Jews so they rebelled, which caused clashes. Palestinian Jews wanted the British to allow more Jews in, so they attacked them to force them to change their minds. They felt that they could not trust the British to help them gain independence, so they started acting violently to try to make them leave.

What are the strengths and weaknesses of Answer A?
The first sentence is very promising. It just needs a little more explanation. The second sentence, however, is not really relevant. The question referred to Palestinian Arabs, not Jews.

Answer B
One cause of the clashes was political. Palestinian Arabs felt that they should have been given independence after the First World War; instead the British now controlled Palestine as a Mandate. Arab demands for independence increased when they saw their neighbours gaining political rights while they had none – Iraq became independent in 1932, for example – and their anger caused clashes with the British. In 1937 (after Peel's Partition Plan was announced) Arab anger escalated into a full-scale revolt against the British. During the revolt, Palestinian Arabs demanded both independence and an end of Jewish migration. This caused clashes between the Arabs and the British because the Arabs felt that Islam was likely to be harmed in the region as more and more Jews arrived. The British weren't doing enough to stop Jewish immigration into Palestine so the Arabs tried to force them to leave.

A second cause of the clashes was therefore religious, and resulted from the Palestinian Muslim reaction to Jewish migration to Palestine. The British encouraged Jewish immigration under the Balfour Declaration. The anger of Palestinian Arabs mounted as the number of Jews arriving increased. In 1929 a violent dispute broke out between the Muslims and Jews over access to the Wailing Wall in Jerusalem: the British police suppressed the dispute harshly and many were killed or injured.

What are the strengths and weaknesses of Answer B?
This is an excellent answer. It gives two causes and provides factual support in showing how those causes brought about the clashes. It would be likely to receive full marks.

Challenge a friend
Use the Student Book to set a part (b) question for a friend. Then look at the answer. Does it do the following things?

☐ Provide two causes
☐ Provide detailed information to support the causes
☐ Show how the causes led to the given outcome.

If it does, you can tell your friend that the answer is very good!

2. THE CREATION OF ISRAEL, THE WAR OF 1948–49 AND THE SUEZ CRISIS OF 1956

LEARNING OBJECTIVES

- Understand why Israel was able to survive the First Arab–Israeli War
- Understand the impact of this war on Palestinians
- Understand the causes and consequences of the Suez Crisis of 1956.

Six months after the UN had voted to partition Palestine, Jewish leader David Ben-Gurion announced the birth of a new state, Israel. Israelis enjoyed just one day of peace. On 15 May 1948, the same day that the last exhausted British troops left, five Arab states invaded, determined to destroy the new state. Israel survived, but the consequences of the First Arab–Israeli War were a disaster for Palestinian Arabs.

The neighbour Israel had the most to fear from was Egypt. It had the biggest population and, from 1954, a new leader, Gamal Abdel Nasser. As Nasser improved Egypt's armed forces, Israeli concerns increased. These concerns led Israel to form a plan with Britain and France to seize control of the Suez Canal in 1956. The Suez Crisis that followed was a disaster for Britain and France, but Israel got the military and economic security it wanted. For Nasser, the Suez Crisis was also a triumph.

2.1 THE FIRST ARAB–ISRAELI WAR, 1948–49

LEARNING OBJECTIVES

- Understand the reasons why Israel survived the First Arab–Israeli War
- Understand the impact of this war on Palestinians
- Understand the reasons for Jewish migration to Israel, and the impact of this.

On 14 May 1948, at 4 p.m., David Ben-Gurion announced the foundation of the state of Israel. The ceremony took just 32 minutes. The USA immediately recognised the new state. A little while later so did the USSR. Arab states immediately denounced it. At midnight on 14 May, the British Mandate ended and, on Saturday 15 May 1948, the last British soldier left Palestine.

The same day, 15 May, the new state was invaded by the armies of five Arab states – Egypt, Syria, Transjordan, Lebanon and Iraq – determined to destroy Israel. The civil war had become an international war.

PHASE 1: MAY–JUNE 1948

In the first 3 weeks of the war, Israel struggled for survival. Only one in three of its troops had weapons, and it had only five field guns. The Arab forces had 152. For a time, it appeared that the new country might be cut in two.
- The Arab Legion, the army of Transjordan, occupied the West Bank and captured east Jerusalem (including the walled Old City, which contained holy sites like Temple Mount and the Wailing Wall).
- Iraqi forces invaded the north.
- Egyptians attacked from the south.

EXTEND YOUR KNOWLEDGE

THE DEFENCE OF YAD MORDECHAI
A clear example of Israel's weakness in this phase, but also the determination and co-ordination of its forces, was the defence of Yad Mordechai. This isolated *kibbutz* (communal farm) was attacked by 2,500 Egyptian troops in May 1948. Just before the attack, 92 women and children were evacuated (moved to a safe place). The remaining 110 settlers, including 20 women, with 40 Palmach (the best-trained section of the Haganah), managed to delay the Egyptians for 5 days before the *kibbutz* fell. The delay gave Israeli forces further north time to organise a defensive line, which prevented the Egyptians taking Tel Aviv.

SOURCE A

David Ben-Gurion proclaims the new state of Israel, 14 May 1948. A picture of Theodor Herzl hangs on the wall behind him (see page 4).

Then, on 11 June, the United Nations intervened. Its negotiator, Count Bernadotte, managed to arrange a month's truce. Without this truce, Israel might not have survived, and it used the time the truce gave it well. It established a military structure with only one man in charge, David Ben-Gurion in Tel Aviv, who gave orders to four regional commands. It also ignored the UN's **embargo** on weapons. Money from Zionist supporters in the USA was used to buy weapons from Czechoslovakia, including 30,000 rifles, 4,500 machine guns, 47 million rounds of ammunition and 84 aeroplanes.

PHASE 2: JULY 1948

Two days before the truce ended, Israeli forces went on the offensive. Surprise was their main weapon. Following intensive fighting around Tel Aviv, Israeli troops occupied the Arab towns of Lydda and Ramleh, and expelled the Arab populations of these towns. A second truce was arranged by the UN. This one lasted for 3 months.

PHASE 3: OCTOBER 1948–JULY 1949

Once again, Israel broke the truce early, this time to gain land before an eventual peace settlement. Israeli forces captured Galilee from the Lebanese and then retook the Negev Desert, pushing the Egyptian forces back into the Sinai Desert. The war then moved slowly to a close when **armistice** agreements were signed with Egypt (February), Lebanon (March), Transjordan (April) and Syria (July). Only Iraq refused to sign one.

THE REASONS FOR ISRAEL'S VICTORY

At first, Israel's chances of winning the war looked very slim. Five states were fighting against one. Put another way, 41 million Arabs faced 650,000 Jews. There were several reasons for the Israeli victory.

1. The Arab states did not send their entire armies to the war. Over-confident, they thought that Israel would be easy to defeat. When the war started, the combined Arab forces sent to attack Israel totalled only about 20–25,000. With about 35,000, Israel's forces were larger. Both sides increased their armies during the war but, by December 1948, Israel's forces had grown to 108,000, double the number of the Arab forces.

2. The Israelis were also much more experienced as fighters than the Arabs. Many Haganah members had served with the British forces in the Second World War, while Irgun and Lehi members had experience fighting against the British. The Israelis were also helped by about 5,000 foreign volunteers, most of whom had military experience. In contrast, only Transjordan had an effective army, the Arab Legion.

3. The first truce called by the UN was absolutely crucial to Israel's survival. Before that, Israel had been dangerously short of weapons and looked as though it would be cut in two. During this truce, while the Arabs did little, Israel regrouped, increased its forces and bought weapons from Czechoslovakia.

4. Israeli tactics were more effective. Attacks were co-ordinated centrally and troops were moved quickly from one part of the country to another as needed. In contrast, the Arab armies were un-coordinated and failed to communicate. There was no single leader and each country had its own reasons for fighting the war. The Transjordan Arab Legion, for example, had been ordered simply to occupy that part of Palestine given to the Arabs, not to attack the lands given to Israel. Their aim, just to take land, was not popular with other Arabs states. This lack of an agreed plan worked to Israel's advantage.

EXTEND YOUR KNOWLEDGE

COUNT BERNADOTTE

Count Bernadotte was a Swede who had negotiated the release of prisoners, including Jews, from the Nazis during the Second World War. During the truce of June 1948, he proposed a peace plan that would have given the Negev Desert to Arabs and permitted Arab refugees to return to their homes. In September 1948, he was assassinated by the militant group Lehi, which accused him of anti-Semitism.

KEY TERM

armistice an agreement to stop fighting until a final peace settlement can be made

CREATION OF ISRAEL — THE MIDDLE EAST, 1917–2012

EXTEND YOUR KNOWLEDGE

TRANSJORDAN'S AIMS
Transjordan went to war to gain the West Bank, not to destroy Israel. In 1950, Jordan (as Transjordan became known) then formally annexed the West Bank. This move was condemned as illegal by other Arab states. In 1952, while on a visit to Jerusalem, Jordan's King Abdullah I was assassinated by a Palestinian Arab.

5 Finally, the Israelis' exceptionally determined fighting spirit helps to explain why they won the war. They knew that defeat meant the destruction of their new country, so they were fighting not just for their lives but also for Israel's right to exist. Perhaps they felt they were also fighting for all the Jews who had died in the Holocaust.

Even before the war had formally ended, the new state had held its first elections and, in January 1949, David Ben-Gurion became the first prime minister of Israel.

EXAM-STYLE QUESTION

AO1 **AO2**

SKILLS ADAPTIVE LEARNING

Explain **two** causes of Israel's success in the First Arab–Israeli War. **(8 marks)**

HINT
Remember that you only have to write about two causes. So choose the two causes that you consider the most important, and that you can support with exact evidence.

THE RESULTS OF THE 1948–49 WAR

1948 700,000 Palestinians flee or are expelled before and during the 1948–49 war

1949 Creation of UNRWA to help Palestinian refugees Reorganisation of the Israeli Defence Forces (IDF)

1950 The Law of Return passed

1949–51 700,000 Jews migrate to Israel

1950–55 Increasing tension between Israel and Egypt

THE IMPACT OF THE WAR ON PALESTINIANS

SOURCE B
A mural painted in 2011 in Gaza. Many Palestinians still own the keys to the homes they left in 1947–49.

CREATION OF ISRAEL
THE MIDDLE EAST, 1917–2012

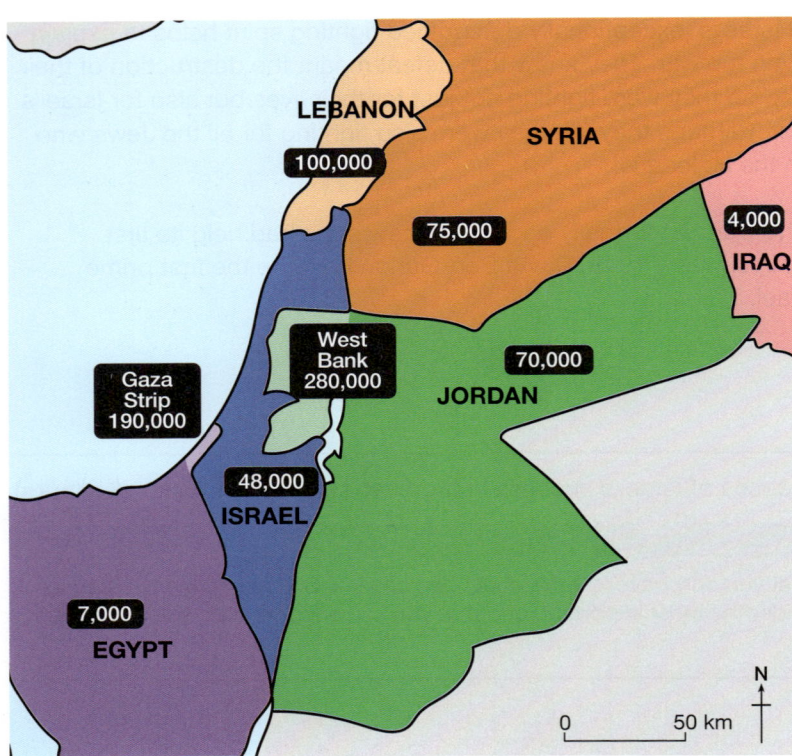

▲ Figure 2.1 A map showing the destinations of the Palestinian refugees, 1947–49. Note that 48,000 Palestinians became refugees within Israel

For Palestinian Arabs, 1948 is *al-Nakba* – 'The Catastrophe'. For them the 1948–49 war was a disaster. In 1947, about 900,000 Arabs lived in the region that became Israel. About 300,000 of these had fled before the war even started in May 1948; a further 400,000 fled during the war. By the end of the war, 700,000 Palestinians had become landless refugees. Even those areas that were meant to be Palestinian Arab, according to the Partition Plan, had been lost, taken over by Israel, Egypt and Jordan (as Transjordan was now called).

Ever since 1949, Palestinians have argued that they have a right to return to their lands. In their view:

- They did not choose to leave their land and they were not told to by Arab leaders.
- The Israelis' aim was an Israel without Arabs: they deliberately set out to expel all Palestinians, and had started this policy (Plan D) before the war started.
- The Israelis achieved their goal by using violence, threats and deliberately causing panic.

The Israeli view was very different.

- Israel did not create the problem: the war was started by the Arabs who invaded Israeli territory on 15 May 1948.
- Palestinians were not forced to leave: they chose to leave or were told to go by Arab leaders. These leaders promised them a quick victory followed by a **triumphal** return, and made up stories of atrocities to frighten them into leaving.
- Palestinians were not permitted to return when the war ended because they would have formed a security threat inside Israel.

SOURCE C

An account by a member of the Haganah in the 1948–49 war. Here he describes what happened in Jerusalem.

An uncontrolled panic swept through all Arab quarters; the Israelis brought up jeeps with loud speakers which broadcast 'horror sounds'. These included shrieks, wails and anguished moans of Arab women, the wail of sirens and the clang of fire alarm bells, interrupted by a… voice calling out in Arabic "Save your souls, all ye faithful: the Jews are using poison gas and atomic weapons. Run for your lives in the name of Allah."

SOURCE D

From an account by an Irish journalist in 1961.

I decided to test the charge that Arab evacuation orders were broadcast by Arab radio – which could be done thoroughly since the BBC monitored all Middle Eastern broadcasts throughout 1948…

There was not a single order, or appeal, or suggestion about evacuation from Palestine from any Arab radio station, inside or outside Palestine in 1948. There is a repeated monitored record of Arab appeals, even flat order, to the civilians of Palestine to stay put.

ACTIVITY

Look at Sources C–D, and read pages 18–20 and 26–27 again.
1 List five reasons why so many Palestinians left their land in 1947–49.
2 If you were a UN investigator, whose view of the Palestinian flight would you support – the Israeli or the Palestinian one? Explain your decision.

CREATION OF ISRAEL — THE MIDDLE EAST, 1917–2012

THE REFUGEE STATUS OF PALESTINIAN ARABS

Whatever had caused Palestinians to leave their homes, the consequences were beyond doubt: Palestinian Arabs no longer had a land of their own and most have remained refugees ever since.

- About 100,000 middle-class Palestinians, many of whom had left before the 1948–49 war even began, started new lives elsewhere in the Middle East, for example in Kuwait, Cairo or Damascus, or migrated to the USA.
- The rest, the vast majority, became refugees in neighbouring states, where they were settled in 54 vast tented camps: four in Jordan; 19 on the West Bank (then occupied by Jordan); 15 in Lebanon; eight in Gaza (then occupied by Egypt); and nine in Syria. Emergency relief was provided by **UNRWA**.

KEY TERMS

UNRWA the United Nations Relief and Works Agency for Palestine Refugees. Set up in 1949, it provides basic services like water and sanitation, health care and education

Arab League an organisation of Arab countries that was set up in 1945, to promote closer relations between Arabs. It originally had six members (those that invaded Israel in 1948, and Saudi Arabia)

The **Arab League** told its members to deny citizenship to Palestinian Arab refugees (and their **descendants**). That way, Palestinians would keep their identity and protect their 'right to return' to their homeland. This meant that, in Lebanon and Egypt, for example, Palestinian refugees found it hard to travel or apply for local jobs. Only Jordan ignored the instruction and granted citizenship to all Palestinians.

Life for those in the eight camps in Gaza was probably the toughest. Gaza is a small strip of land just 45 km long and 8 km wide. The original population was about 20,000. The arrival of 190,000 refugees resulted in overcrowding, water shortages, poor sanitation and a collapse of the local economy.

Many refugees tried to return home to collect their possessions or to harvest their crops. About 16,000 cases of this sort of **infiltration** had occurred by 1953, mostly from Jordanian territory. It was risky because Israeli troops were under orders to stop them by any means necessary.

THE GROWTH OF PALESTINIAN RESISTANCE

KEY TERM

Fedayeen an Arabic word meaning 'those who sacrifice themselves'. Fedayeen were Palestinian freedom fighters or terrorists, depending on one's point of view

Feelings of bewilderment and shock soon turned to bitter hatred and some Palestinians began infiltrations that were aimed at attacking Jews. Between 1950 and 1953, 153 Israelis died and 202 were injured as a result of the missions of these **Fedayeen**. Israel always retaliated fiercely. In October 1953, for example, Israeli troops attacked Qibya in the West Bank, killing 69 villagers and destroying 45 houses, as a reprisal for the death of three Israelis. To stop the cycle of violence, the Jordanian authorities worked to prevent infiltrations from the West Bank in 1954. However, infiltrations continued from Gaza, which was under Egyptian control.

THE IMPACT OF THE WAR ON ISRAELIS

For Israelis, 1948 is their Year of Liberation and the 1948–49 war is their War of Independence, which they see as an extraordinary victory and a triumph. 6,000 Israelis had died, but the new state of Israel had survived. It had kept the land given to it under the Partition Plan and had also captured 50 per cent of the area given to the Arab state. The new state of Israel was now easier to defend, had additional fertile land and had access to Jerusalem. Ignoring the UN Partition Plan (and the fact that Jordanian troops occupied the east of the city), Jerusalem was declared the capital of Israel.

30 CREATION OF ISRAEL — THE MIDDLE EAST, 1917–2012

▶ Figure 2.2 A map of the ceasefire lines showing Israeli gains

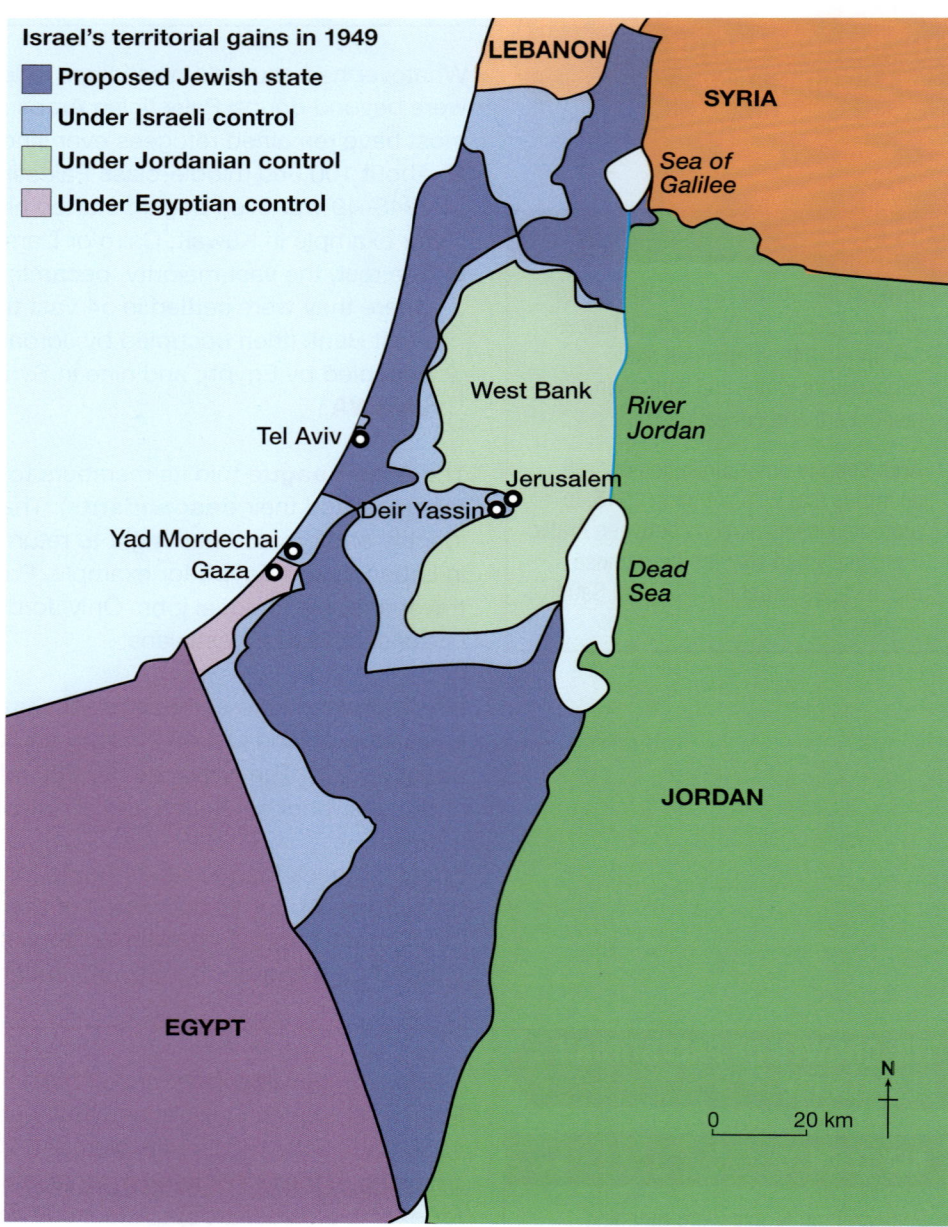

THE LAW OF RETURN, 1950

EXTEND YOUR KNOWLEDGE

THE KNESSET
The Knesset is the name of the Israeli Parliament, which has 120 elected members. Today, the Knesset is housed in a building in Jerusalem that was financed by James Armand de Rothschild, an English Jew, at the then massive sum of 6 million Israeli pounds. Before that was completed in 1966, the Knesset met in several places, including a cinema in Tel Aviv.

The new state of Israel had a very small population. Over the next 3 years this was almost doubled to 1.5 million by the arrival of large numbers of Jewish immigrants. The first group came from Europe. Some were Holocaust survivors from camps in Germany. Many more were Eastern Europeans, seeking a new life away from Soviet control. Large numbers then came from Arab countries where growing anti-Semitism following the 1948–49 war was making life dangerous. All this immigration was supported by the Knesset, which passed the Law of Return in July 1950. This said that any Jew in the world had the right to come to Israel and become an Israeli citizen.

CREATION OF ISRAEL — THE MIDDLE EAST, 1917–2012

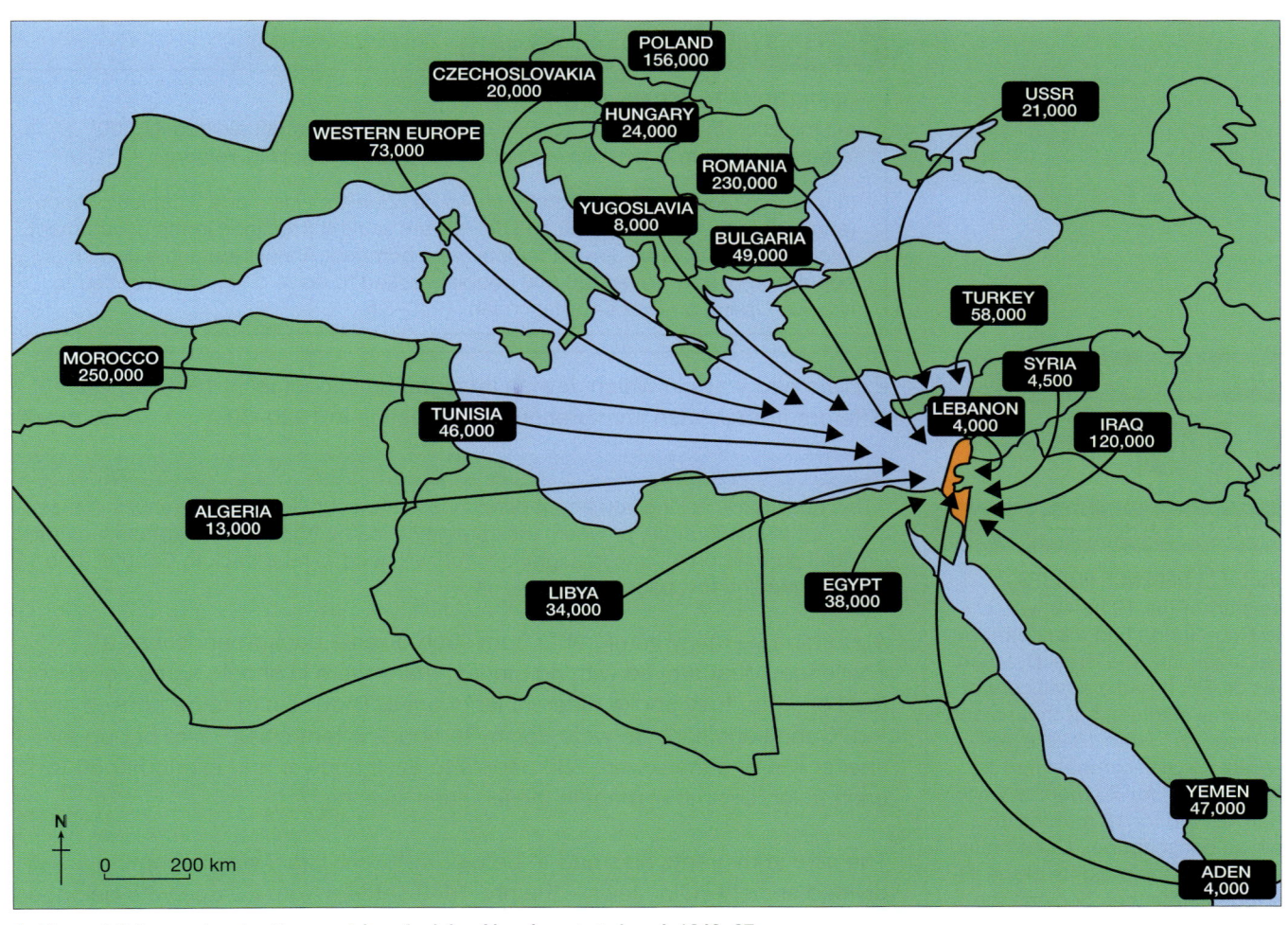

▲ Figure 2.3 A map showing the countries of origin of immigrants to Israel, 1948–67

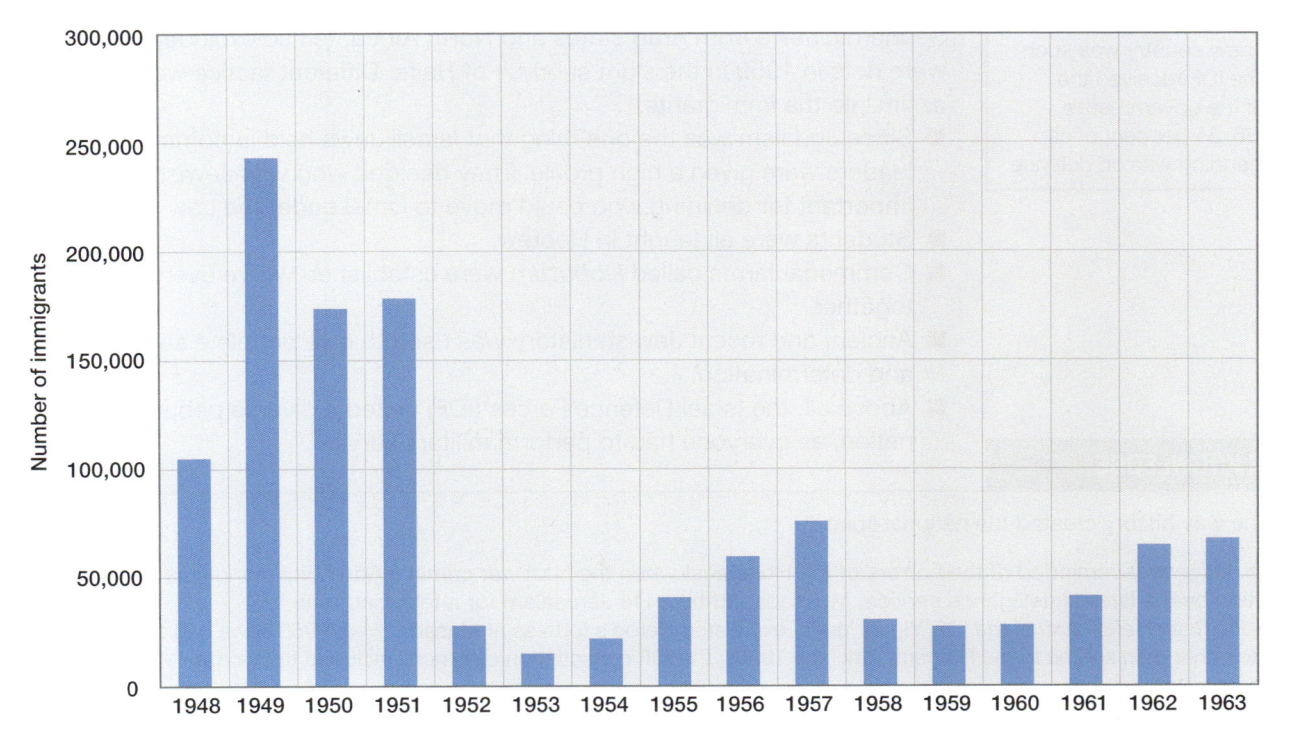

Countries of origin and numbers:
- Poland: 156,000
- Czechoslovakia: 20,000
- Hungary: 24,000
- Western Europe: 73,000
- Romania: 230,000
- Yugoslavia: 8,000
- Bulgaria: 49,000
- USSR: 21,000
- Turkey: 58,000
- Syria: 4,500
- Lebanon: 4,000
- Iraq: 120,000
- Morocco: 250,000
- Tunisia: 46,000
- Algeria: 13,000
- Libya: 34,000
- Egypt: 38,000
- Yemen: 47,000
- Aden: 4,000

▲ Figure 2.4 A graph showing immigration to Israel, 1948–63

Year	Number of immigrants (approx.)
1948	105,000
1949	245,000
1950	175,000
1951	180,000
1952	27,000
1953	15,000
1954	22,000
1955	40,000
1956	60,000
1957	77,000
1958	30,000
1959	27,000
1960	28,000
1961	42,000
1962	65,000
1963	68,000

CREATION OF ISRAEL — THE MIDDLE EAST, 1917–2012

EXTEND YOUR KNOWLEDGE

OPERATIONS TO ESCAPE ANTI-SEMITISM

In Operation Magic Carpet, 1949–50, US and British aircraft airlifted 47,000 Yemenite Jews to Israel following violent anti-Semitic riots in Yemen.

In Iraq also, Jews were blamed for *al-Nakba*. Zionism was made a capital offence (punishable by death) in 1950 and Jews were sacked from jobs in the government. There was panic when Jewish targets were bombed. Almost the entire Jewish population of Iraq – over 120,000 people – asked to leave. They were airlifted to Israel in Operation Ezra and Nehemiah, 1950–51.

EXAM-STYLE QUESTION

A01 **A02**

Explain **two** ways in which Jewish immigration into Israel in 1948–52 was different from Jewish immigration into Palestine in 1920–39. **(6 marks)**

HINT

This question is asking you about differences. You could look at differences in the amount of immigration, or where the immigrants came from, or who authorised (gave official permission for) the immigration. You will need to refer back to Chapter 1 as well as reading this page carefully.

EXTEND YOUR KNOWLEDGE

THE ISRAELI DEFENCE FORCES

At the start of the 1948–49 war, David Ben-Gurion had transformed the Haganah into the Israel Defence Forces or IDF. It had a small core of professional soldiers, but the majority were 'reserves'. From 1949, every non-Arab 18-year-old male had to serve in the IDF for 30 months while females served for 18 months (this is known as conscription). Conscripted troops formed the majority of the IDF. All ex-conscripts then became the reserve forces, expected to train for a month every year until they were 55.

Defending the new country was such a priority that the IDF received the largest share of the government's budget. By 1956, 35 per cent of all government spending was on defence.

Absorbing so many immigrants from such diverse backgrounds was a challenge. Most arrived with no money; many were in shock; some could not read or write; they spoke different languages. They all had to be housed and fed. Conditions early on were harsh. Temporary 'tent cities' were put up for shelter – in one there were 350 people to each shower and in another 56 to each toilet. Unemployment in these 'cities' was high.

The new immigrants also had to be **assimilated**. Israel was becoming a very divided society. 'Old' Jews – the pre-1949 settlers from Europe who belonged to the Ashkenazi branch of Judaism – dominated all the important positions in politics, the military and employment. The 'new' Jews, such as Mizrahi and Sephardic Jews from Arab states and North Africa, felt so excluded that there were riots in 1959 in the slum suburbs of Haifa. Different tactics were used to assimilate the immigrants.

- Since Judaism was the one thing that Israeli Jews held in common, religious leaders were given a high profile. They decided who was Jewish, which was important for deciding who could move to Israel under the Law of Return.
- Students were all taught in Hebrew.
- Communal farms called *kibbutzim* were established where everyone worked together.
- Ancient and recent Jewish history was used to give people a sense of unity and determination.
- Above all, the Israel Defence Forces (IDF) united a diverse people into one nation, as everyone had to perform military service.

EXTEND YOUR KNOWLEDGE

Examples of the way history created the national spirit.

- In 1961, the nation was reminded of the horrors of the Holocaust when the Nazi war criminal Adolf Eichmann was abducted from Argentina by the Israeli intelligence service, Mossad, and taken to Jerusalem for a televised trial.
- In 1963–65, the first chief of staff of the IDF, Yigael Yadin, excavated Herod's fortress at Masada, where 960 Jews had committed mass suicide rather than submit to the Romans. Until the 1990s, the IDF conscription ceremony included the words, 'Masada shall not fall again'.
- Using history also involved editing out references to an Arabic past in Palestine. By 1950, about 200 Arabic place names had been changed, and empty Palestinian homes were destroyed or given to Jewish immigrants.

ISRAEL'S RELATIONS WITH EGYPT

Israel's struggle to survive economically was made more difficult because the Arab League boycotted all trade with Israel, and also boycotted any foreign company trading with Israel. Egypt searched all ships using the Suez Canal, confiscating any items they thought had been purchased at an Israeli port or that might be bound for Israel's armed forces. From 1951, Egypt also starting making life difficult for foreign ships that were heading up the Gulf of Aqaba towards Israel's southern port of Eilat. Since the Straits of Tiran, at the entrance of this gulf, were dominated by the Egyptian town of Sharm el Sheikh, this was easy to do. Although Egypt controlled Gaza, it also did nothing to stop the Fedayeen raids on Israel from there.

Relations then got even worse because of events inside Egypt, when the weak King Farouk was eventually replaced by a dynamic new leader, Nasser.

2.2 THE SUEZ CRISIS OF 1956

LEARNING OBJECTIVES

- Understand the reasons why Nasser's ambitions and actions caused mounting concern in Britain, France and Israel
- Understand the terms of the Sèvres Agreement and the events of the Suez Crisis
- Understand the results of the Suez Crisis.

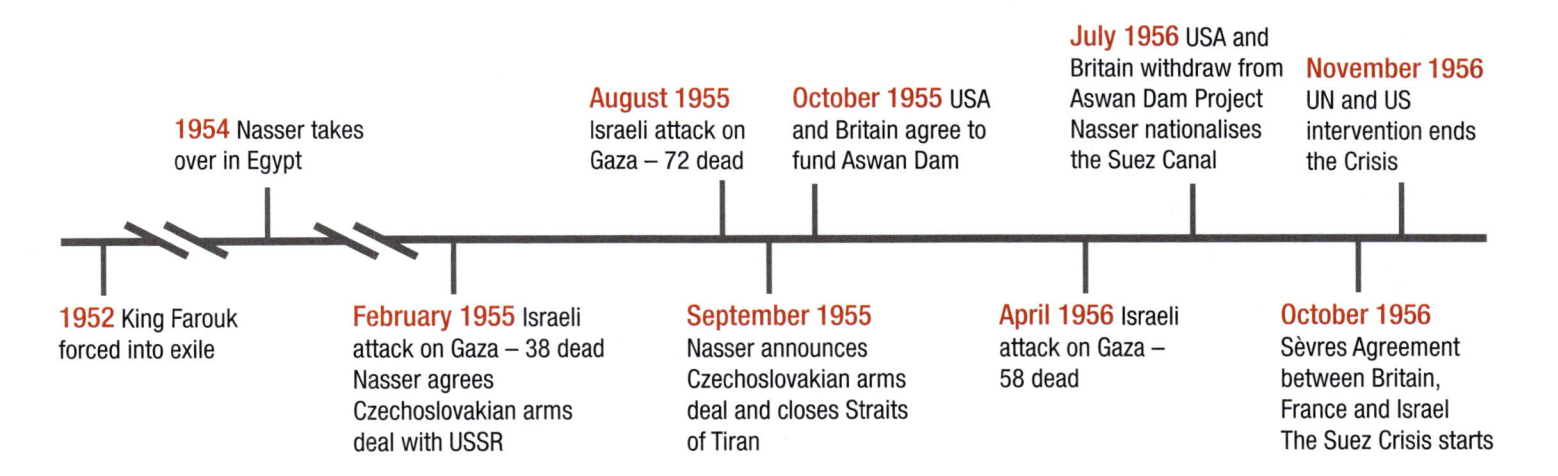

1952 King Farouk forced into exile

1954 Nasser takes over in Egypt

February 1955 Israeli attack on Gaza – 38 dead Nasser agrees Czechoslovakian arms deal with USSR

August 1955 Israeli attack on Gaza – 72 dead

September 1955 Nasser announces Czechoslovakian arms deal and closes Straits of Tiran

October 1955 USA and Britain agree to fund Aswan Dam

April 1956 Israeli attack on Gaza – 58 dead

July 1956 USA and Britain withdraw from Aswan Dam Project Nasser nationalises the Suez Canal

October 1956 Sèvres Agreement between Britain, France and Israel The Suez Crisis starts

November 1956 UN and US intervention ends the Crisis

King Farouk of Egypt had a reputation as a **playboy**. He was only 16 when he became king in 1936 and he used his vast wealth to enjoy a lavish lifestyle. He owned dozens of palaces and cars, and 1,000 suits. While most Egyptians lived in poverty, he indulged in rich banquets and spent lavishly on his jewel and coin collections. Egyptians became increasingly frustrated with his incompetent and corrupt government. They also disliked that fact that Farouk did nothing to remove British involvement in Egyptian affairs. 80,000 British troops were still in the country, guarding the Suez Canal, even though Egypt had been an independent state for many years and there was no longer any threat of a Nazi invasion.

CREATION OF ISRAEL

Egypt's defeat by Israel in the 1948–49 war triggered Farouk's removal. He was personally blamed for his troops' lack of preparation and faulty weapons. In 1952, the 32-year-old king was forced to abdicate by a group of disillusioned army officers.

ACTIVITY

To help you understand this section, label a blank map with the following:
- Countries: Israel, Egypt
- Places: Cairo, Sharm el Sheikh, Aswan, Sinai, Gaza
- Seas: Mediterranean, Red Sea
- Waterways: River Nile, Suez Canal, Straits of Tiran

Now shade in the areas controlled by Israel and Egypt in 1952.

NASSER AND EGYPT'S LEADERSHIP OF THE ARAB WORLD

In 1954, one of these army officers, Colonel Gamal Abdel Nasser, took over the government. Nasser had ambitious dreams:

▶ Figure 2.5 Nasser's three dreams

Complete independence: He wanted to free Egypt from British 'occupation'.

Prosperity: He wanted to improve the lives of ordinary Egyptians.

Pride: He wanted Arabs everywhere to be proud of themselves and to believe in their united strength.

He achieved the first ambition quickly. Britain agreed that its troops would withdraw from the Suez Canal zone. They agreed to return only if another country attacked the Canal.

Nasser then began his programme of internal reform. Most Egyptians lived in poverty, while a privileged few owned most of the arable land (land used for farming). Nasser planned to redistribute this land to the **peasants**, and to build schools and hospitals. He also aimed to dam the River Nile at Aswan in order to control the Nile's annual floods, and to provide hydroelectric power and water for **irrigation**. He asked the USA and Britain to lend him the money needed for the dam. They were keen for any ally against the USSR, and so they opened talks about the loan.

However, when Nasser began to work on his third ambition, the West started to have concerns. Nasser's broadcasts on Cairo Radio were heard by millions of Arabs. He wanted all Arab states to be proudly independent and neutral in the Cold War. He soon became the champion of **Arab nationalism**. But, if Egypt was going to lead and defend a united Arab world, Nasser would need to purchase modern weapons. He asked the USA, but they refused because they thought he would use the weapons against Israel.

KEY TERM

Arab nationalism the main goal of Arab nationalism was to achieve Arab independence, first from the Ottomans, and now from Britain and France. Some Arab nationalists wanted to create a single Arab state that would unite all the Arabs of North Africa and the Middle East. Other Arab governments did not agree with this aim, but they were united in their hatred of Israel

CREATION OF ISRAEL — THE MIDDLE EAST, 1917–2012

THE IMPACT OF ISRAELI ATTACKS ON GAZA, 1955

Humiliating proof of Egypt's military weakness came in February 1955 when the IDF launched a massive raid on an Egyptian army headquarters in Gaza, killing 38 Egyptian soldiers. The IDF claimed it was a reprisal for the killing of a cyclist in Israel by Palestinian militants, one of whom carried documents linking him with Egyptian intelligence.

The Egyptian public demanded revenge and Palestinians in Gaza rioted, chanting, 'Give us weapons'. Nasser needed to act if he was to keep his image as the strongest leader of the Arab world. He negotiated a secret arms deal with Czechoslovakia, a Soviet ally. In return for $300 million of Egyptian cotton, Egypt was rearmed with massive Soviet firepower: 100 self-propelled guns, 200 armoured personnel carriers, 300 tanks, 200 MIG-15 fighters and 50 bombers.

In August 1955, a Fedayeen raid killed 11 Israelis; the IDF reprisal attack on Gaza left 72 Egyptian soldiers dead. In response, Nasser made public the Czechoslovakian arms deal. He also imposed a complete blockade on all trade through the Straits of Tiran. His popularity in Egypt had never been higher: he was standing up to Israel.

In two critical respects, though, Nasser's actions **backfired**.

- Israel decided war against Egypt was inevitable and it would be better to fight sooner rather than wait until Nasser's new Soviet weapons had arrived. In November 1955, an IDF attack on Gaza killed 50 Egyptian soldiers and, in April 1956, an Israeli mortar attack on Gaza caused 58 civilian deaths. However, these efforts didn't provoke Egypt into a war.
- News that Egypt was purchasing large quantities of Soviet weapons caused shock and concern in the West. In October 1955, the USA and Britain offered to loan Egypt $270 million for the Aswan Dam. They hoped to win Egypt back from an **alliance** with the USSR. But that failed to happen and, in July 1956, the USA and Britain suddenly took back their offer. Perhaps they hoped this tactic would make Nasser rethink his Soviet alliance.

NASSER NATIONALISES THE SUEZ CANAL

Nasser's response a week later came as a shock: he **nationalised** the Suez Canal. He said that he would compensate the shareholders and use the toll money from the Canal to build the Aswan Dam. His action was greeted with delight throughout the Arab world, but with furious protests from Britain and France. Both considered the action illegal, and a major threat to their trade and position in the Middle East.

> **EXTEND YOUR KNOWLEDGE**
>
> **WHY DID ISRAEL ATTACK GAZA?**
> Israel was not a priority for Nasser and he had made an effort to keep the border quiet, so the scale of Israeli actions against Gaza in 1955–56 is puzzling. One suggestion is that David Ben-Gurion feared a united Arab front led by Nasser, and the development of close ties between the USA and Egypt. If he could expose Nasser as weak, it would undermine him in Arab eyes. If he could push Nasser into asking the USSR for help, it would damage US–Egyptian relations. Ben-Gurion may also have wanted to provoke an Egyptian response in order to justify Israel's high military expenditure in a time of economic difficulty.

> **KEY TERM**
>
> **nationalise** to transfer control of something (e.g. a company) from private to state ownership. So the Canal was now owned by the Egyptian government

> **ACTIVITY**
>
> 1. Imagine that you are the editor of an Egyptian newspaper. Under a bold headline, write a paragraph praising Nasser's nationalisation of the Suez Canal. You could explain how this action will help Nasser to achieve his dreams for Egypt.
> 2. Now imagine that you are the editor of a British newspaper. Under an equally bold headline, write a paragraph explaining why you strongly condemn Nasser's nationalisation of the Suez Canal.

SOURCE E

Crowds cheer Nasser following his nationalisation of the Suez Canal, 1956.

Britain, France and Israel were united in their anger against Egypt, and had growing concerns about Nasser's popularity and new military strength. They decided to work together.

NASSER'S MOTIVES FOR NATIONALISING THE SUEZ CANAL

It was the decision of the USA and Britain to withdraw the loan to build the Aswan Dam that led to Nasser nationalising the Canal. He wanted to show Britain and France that he did not need their support and he could find his own resources to build the dam.

But he had other motives too.
- He wanted to show that he was the leader of the Arab world and to promote Arab nationalism.
- He wanted to gain full independence for Egypt and break free from British colonialism. Egypt's future should be decided by Egyptians, not the West.
- He was keen to improve Egypt's economy and the lives of its people. The Aswan Dam would provide irrigation and hydro-electricity to boost agriculture. Nationalising the Suez Canal would provide Nasser with his own funds to build the dam.

THE SÈVRES AGREEMENT

In secret, David Ben-Gurion and Moshe Dayan, the head of the IDF, flew to France on 22 October 1956. At an isolated house outside Sèvres, they met with French and British ministers. Over the next 3 days, a plan was made: Israel would attack Egypt; Britain and France could then invade Egypt, while pretending to keep the peace. If the plan succeeded, Israel's security and ability to trade would be assured, while Britain and France would regain control of the Suez Canal. All three hoped to overthrow Nasser.

THE SUEZ CRISIS, 1956

The Sèvres Agreement was immediately put into action. On 29 October 1956, Israel invaded Egypt, occupied Gaza and dropped paratroopers into Sinai, near the Suez Canal. A further 1,000 men in 200 vehicles set off for Sharm el Sheikh

CREATION OF ISRAEL
THE MIDDLE EAST, 1917–2012

across almost 300 km of desert. On 30 October, Britain and France ordered Israel and Egypt to stop fighting and to withdraw 16 km either side of the Canal. As predicted, Nasser refused. So, in early November, Britain and France launched an airborne attack, defeating Egyptian forces and advancing towards the Suez Canal. Meanwhile, Israel had taken control of Sharm el Sheikh and ended the blockade. From a military point of view, everything seemed to be going well, except that Nasser sank ships in the Suez Canal to block it.

However, from a political point of view, the action of Britain and France was a failure. On 6 November, UN Secretary General Dag Hammarskjöld called a ceasefire. The American president, Dwight Eisenhower, was highly critical of the attack and the USSR threatened to intervene on Egypt's side. Britain, France and Israel were forced to withdraw their troops from Egypt and a UN peacekeeping force was sent in to supervise the ceasefire. The whole crisis had lasted only 8 days, but it had a powerful impact.

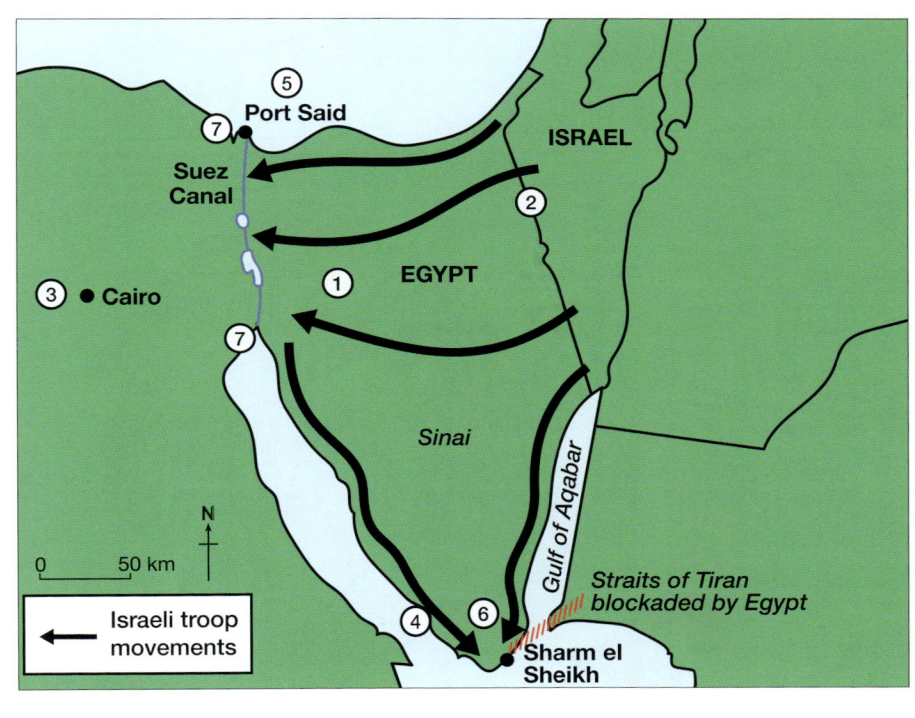

① 29 October
Israeli paratroopers land east of Suez Canal.

30 October
Britain and France order Israel and Egypt to withdraw their troops 16 km on each side of the Suez Canal. Israel accepts, but Egypt refuses.

② 30 October–5 November
Israeli troops advance across Sinai.

③ 31 October
British and French bomb Egyptian airfields.

④ 2 November
Israeli paratroopers dropped near Al Tor.

⑤ 5–6 November
British and French forces invade Port Said and move inland to take control of the Suez Canal.

⑥ 5 November
Israeli soldiers capture Sharm el Sheikh and lift the blockade on the Straits of Tiran.

⑦ 5 November
Nasser sinks ships to block the Canal.

6 November
Britain and France strongly criticised by USA & USSR. Britain and France agree to UN ceasefire.

▲ Figure 2.6 The Suez Crisis

EXAM-STYLE QUESTION

A01 A02

SKILLS ADAPTIVE LEARNING

Explain **two** causes of the Suez Crisis of 1956. **(8 marks)**

HINT
This question is asking you about causation. You could explain the causes of the Suez Crisis from two angles – the reasons why the Israelis decided to attack, and the reasons for British and French involvement.

RESULTS OF THE SUEZ CRISIS

■ The short campaign was a success for Israel. It gained no land since it had to withdraw from Sinai and Gaza, but it had achieved both of its objectives: security and the ability to trade. Egypt's military strength had been temporarily wrecked, Fedayeen bases had been destroyed, and the blockade on the Straits of Tiran had been lifted. The IDF had also shown that it could beat an Arab state and it had captured many weapons. UN peacekeepers were sent to Sinai to keep the peace on the Egyptian–Israeli border, which added to Israel's sense of security. Morale in Israel was higher than ever.

- For Britain and France, however, the Suez Crisis was a humiliating disaster. They had failed to remove Nasser or to regain control of the Suez Canal. By using such underhand tactics, the international reputation of both countries was damaged. They were also now seen as allies of Israel and therefore lost influence with other Middle East countries. The crisis caused deep political divisions in Britain and France, and the British prime minister, Anthony Eden, resigned.

SOURCE F

A Soviet cartoon showing Egypt as a sphinx and a defeated British lion and French cockerel. The sphinx has the lion's tail in its paws.

ACTIVITY

Study Source F.
1 What do you think the cartoonist is trying to say?
2 Do you think it is an accurate message or is there any reason to doubt it?

- The Crisis marked the arrival of the world's two **superpowers** on the Middle Eastern stage. The USSR now had a firm ally in the area, Egypt, which looked to it for protection. Meanwhile, the USA emerged as the most important Western power in the region, as Britain and France had been humiliated and forced to back down by the Americans.
- Egypt gained from the crisis. Nasser now had complete control of the Suez Canal (the sunken ships only took 6 months to remove). The USSR agreed to finance the Aswan Dam, so Nasser was also able to go ahead with his plans to improve life for Egyptians. With Soviet support, he was also able to rebuild his armed forces. However, life became very difficult for Egypt's 40,000 Jews. Nasser seized Jewish businesses and banned Jews from working as teachers, lawyers or doctors. About 25,000 Jews migrated as a result.

CREATION OF ISRAEL — THE MIDDLE EAST, 1917–2012

SOURCE G

Nasser and the Soviet leader, Nikita Khrushchev, open the Aswan Dam, 1964.

ACTIVITY

When historians consider the significance of an event, they ask questions like 'How deeply were people's lives affected by the event?', 'How many people were affected by it?', 'Was the impact just local, or wider than that?', and 'Did the event cause a stir at the time? Is it still remembered today?'

To work out the significance of the Suez Crisis, it helps to understand the situation before and after the event. Draw a table with two columns and three rows. Label the columns 'Before the Suez Crisis' and 'After the Suez Crisis'. Label the rows 'Israel's security', 'Egypt's strength', and 'Britain's influence'.

1. Fill in the table using the information in this section.
2. Which country was the most affected by the Suez Crisis? How did you decide?
3. In your view, does the Suez Crisis count as an event of major significance? Give three reasons for your view.

- Nasser's gains from Suez extended beyond Egypt. He was hailed as a hero by other Arab states for standing up to the bullying tactics of the British and French. In 1958, he was invited by Syria to join their two countries to form a United Arab Republic, with Nasser as the first president. Some Arabs hoped that the UAR would be the first step towards creating an Arab state that would unite all the Arabs of North Africa and the Middle East. When Nasser visited the Syrian capital, Damascus, in February 1958, he was cheered by massive crowds. The UAR experiment did not last, since Syria withdrew in 1961 (it disliked being the junior partner), but the fact that it had been proposed at all was a measure of Nasser's popularity and importance in the Arab world.
- Of course, the Suez Crisis did not solve the underlying dispute between Israel and its neighbours – Israel's right to exist. Though Nasser now focused on internal reforms, Syria was as determined as ever to destroy Israel.

THE ATTITUDES OF THE SUPERPOWERS

Both the USSR and the USA had a keen interest in the events in Egypt. At this time they were involved in a Cold War and each of them was determined to maintain an influence in the region. The USSR had already increased its standing in Egypt by allowing its ally, Czechoslovakia, to supply Soviet weapons. When the attack on the Canal took place, the USA criticised what Britain and France had done and called a United Nations Security Council meeting to condemn the attack. Although the USA did not lose face over what happened, the USSR gained influence as the Western allies squabbled among themselves over what had happened.

RECAP

RECALL QUIZ

1. When did the British finally leave Palestine?
2. Name the five states that invaded Israel in 1948.
3. Give two reasons why Israel was so successful in the First Arab–Israeli War.
4. Give two reasons for the flight of Palestinians in the period 1947–49.
5. What was UNRWA?
6. Give two reasons why Israel passed the Law of Return.
7. In what year did each of the following happen: the overthrow of King Farouk of Egypt; Nasser becomes leader of Egypt; Nasser nationalises the Suez Canal?
8. Why did the USA and Britain withdraw their offer to finance the Aswan Dam?
9. Give four ways in which Egypt changed in the period 1954–56.
10. Give two consequences of the Suez Crisis for Israel.

CHECKPOINT

STRENGTHEN
S1 Explain two ways in which the state of Israel by 1949 was different from the Jewish state that the Partition Plan of 1947 had proposed.
S2 Explain the importance of: the Straits of Tiran to Israel; the Suez Canal to Britain; the Aswan Dam to Egypt.
S3 What did the USSR gain from the Suez Crisis?

CHALLENGE
C1 How far was the UN responsible for Israel's success in the 1948–49 war?
C2 How far did Israel change in the years 1948 to 1956?
C3 How far were the USA and USSR responsible for change in the Middle East in 1947–56?

SUMMARY

- In May 1948, after the British withdrew, five Arab states invaded the newly created state of Israel. This led to the Arab–Israeli War, 1948–49.
- By 1949, Israel had survived and captured more land, but 700,000 Palestinians had become refugees.
- Surrounded by enemies, Israel focused on defence and increasing its population.
- Nasser took over in Egypt in 1954 and his plans for reform were supported by the West.
- However, when he bought Soviet weapons, America and Britain withdrew support for his Aswan Dam project.
- To raise money, Nasser took over the Suez Canal, which infuriated Britain and France.
- Israel was concerned by Egypt's behaviour over the Straits of Tiran and its military strength.
- In October 1956, Britain, France and Israel conspired together to attack Egypt.
- The Suez Crisis lasted 8 days: though Israel achieved its goals, Britain and France were humiliated.
- Egypt gained from the Suez Crisis: Nasser was now seen as a hero in the Arab world and, with Soviet help, Egypt built the Aswan Dam and rearmed.

CREATION OF ISRAEL — THE MIDDLE EAST, 1917–2012

EXAM GUIDANCE: PART (C) QUESTIONS

A01 **A02**

SKILLS PROBLEM SOLVING, REASONING, DECISION MAKING

Question to be answered: How far was Britain responsible for increased violence in the Middle East in the period 1917–47?

You may use the following in your answer:
- the Peel Commission
- the Jewish insurgency

You must also use information of your own.   (16 marks)

1 Analysis Question 1: What is the question type testing?

In this question you have to demonstrate that you have knowledge and understanding of the key features and characteristics of the period studied. In this particular case it is knowledge and understanding of the role of Britain in the period 1917–47 and how there was an increase in violence in the region.

You also have to explain, analyse and make judgements about historical events and periods to give an explanation and reach a judgement on the role of various factors in bringing about changes.

2 Analysis Question 2: What do I have to do to answer the question well?

- You have been given two factors on which to write: you don't have to use those factors (though it might be wise to do so). You must, however, include at least one factor, other than those you have been given.
- That factor might be the terms of the Mandate, or the Nazi policies in Germany in the 1930s.
- But you must avoid just giving the information. What changes did these events cause?
- You are also asked 'how far' Britain was responsible for the change. So, when discussing these events, you need to consider whether it was Britain that was causing the change.

3 Analysis Question 3: Are there any techniques I can use to make it very clear that I am doing what is needed to be successful?

This is a 16-mark question and you need to make sure you give a substantial answer. You will be up against time pressures so some useful techniques to help you succeed might be.
- Don't write a long introduction. Give a brief introduction that answers the question straight away and shows what your paragraphs are going to be about.
- To make sure you stay focused on the question and avoid just writing narrative, try to use the words of the question at the beginning of each paragraph.
- Remember this question is a causation question, so (as in Question b) make sure what you are writing about explains why this did or did not mean Britain caused change.

CREATION OF ISRAEL — THE MIDDLE EAST, 1917–2012

Answer
Here is a student response with teacher comments.

This period was one where there was an increase in violence in the Middle East. A major cause of this was a hardening of attitudes between Jews and Palestinians and in how both those groups viewed the British. British policies in this period were partly responsible for this change, but some factors (e.g. the impact of Nazi policies) were not the responsibility of the British.

Good introduction.

There was a change in the amount of violence in this period and Britain was responsible for much of this violence, especially up to 1948. For example, the British government issued the Balfour Declaration, which agreed to the use of Palestine as a Jewish homeland; Britain then allowed Jewish immigration to Palestine in the 1920s and 1930s. This resulted in considerable tension and increasing levels of violence as Palestinian Arabs resented the fact that they had not been granted independence at the end of the First World War. They blamed Britain for this, and even more deeply resented the fact that they had not been consulted about Jewish immigration. They felt they were being swamped, so they turned to violence to show their discontent and to try to get the British to change their mind.

Nice paragraph. Answers the question, gives contextual knowledge and links violence to British actions.

Arab resentment escalated from clashes with Jews into a full scale revolt when Britain published the Peel Commission's proposal to partition Palestine, an idea Arabs rejected. However, Britain's decision to shelve the Peel proposals in 1939 and then its decision to strictly limit Jewish migration after the Second World War upset the Jews in the region and caused an increase in Jewish terrorism. Gangs like the Irgun and Lehi were determined to force a change of policy on Britain. In October 1945, they blew up the Palestine railway system and, over the next 3 years, they killed British troops, bombed airfields and bridges, and targeted 'anything British'. They even blew up the British headquarters at the King David Hotel in Jerusalem in July 1946.

Good detail, linking violence back to a British decision. However, you do need to refer to this violence as the 'Jewish insurgency' in order to make the link to the question explicit.

However, there were definitely some causes of violence in the region that were not Britain's fault. For example, Britain could not be blamed for what happened as a result of the impact of the anti-Jewish policies adopted by the Nazis in the 1930s. That had a major impact on events in Palestine.

This is a very disappointing paragraph. Can you say what those policies were? You need to mention how they led to increased immigration, British controls, Jewish terrorism and perhaps the Holocaust and US Zionist pressure. Is any of that Britain's fault?

In conclusion, Britain was responsible for much of the increased violence because of policies such as the Balfour Declaration and Peel Commission, but not for tension created as a result of Nazi policies.

Good concise finish.

Work with a friend
Discuss with a friend how you would turn the weaker paragraphs in the answer to ones that would enable the whole answer to get very high marks.
Does your answer do the following?

- ☐ Identify causes
- ☐ Provide detailed information to support the causes
- ☐ Show how the causes led to the given outcome
- ☐ Provide factors other than those given in the question
- ☐ Address 'how far?'

3. TENSION AND CONFLICT, 1956–73

LEARNING OBJECTIVES

- Understand the causes, key events and consequences of the Six Day War, 1967
- Understand the development and impact of Palestinian resistance
- Understand the causes, key events and impact of the Yom Kippur War, 1973.

On 5 June 1967, the world awoke to the stunning news that Israel had launched surprise attacks on the air forces of Egypt, Syria and Jordan. Over the next 6 days, Israel completely defeated the forces of its Arab neighbours and took land that increased its size by 350 per cent. This land – the occupied territories – has been an issue and a source of conflict ever since.

The 1967 war also marked a turning point for Palestinians. Many fled the war zone and moved to grim refugee camps in surrounding countries. Palestinian militants now abandoned their policy of relying on Arab nations to destroy Israel. They would do the job themselves. Support for Palestinian guerrilla groups soared and Israel experienced a growing number of ever more violent attacks. Other Palestinian militants turned to international terrorism – hijacking planes, for example – to draw the world's attention to the plight of the Palestinians. These tactics backfired when the PLO were thrown out of Jordan in 1970.

Meanwhile, Egypt's determination to recover the Sinai led to the war of 1973. On Yom Kippur, the Jewish Day of Atonement, Syria and Egypt launched a brilliantly co-ordinated, well-armed attack on the Israeli front lines in Sinai and the Golan Heights. This time, Israel was taken by surprise. Although the exceptional quality of the IDF meant Israel was able to push back the assaults, the war threatened to involve the superpowers and saw the first use of the 'oil weapon'.

3.1 TENSION

LEARNING OBJECTIVES
- Understand the Arab states' aims concerning Israel
- Understand the reasons for growing tension between Israel, Syria and Jordan
- Understand the actions of the USSR and Egypt leading up to the Six Day War.

May 1964 PLO set up

November 1966 Egypt and Syria sign a defence pact (agreement)

April 1967 Dogfight between Israeli and Syrian fighter planes

January 1964 Cairo Conference: Arab states commit to the destruction of Israel

January 1965 Yasser Arafat and Fatah achieve publicity with a failed terrorist attack

November 1966 Samu Incident between Israel and Jordan

May 1967 Nasser orders the UN to leave Sinai; he also closes the Straits of Tiran Egypt and Jordan sign a defence pact

NASSER AND ARAB AIMS – THE CAIRO CONFERENCE, 1964

After the 1956 Suez Crisis, Nasser enjoyed his reputation as the leader of the Arab world. However, the United Arab Republic idea had not worked and Syria had pulled out of the alliance in 1961. Syria was now also stealing the headlines because of a dispute with Israel over who controlled the sources of the River Jordan. Determined to show his leadership of the Arab world once more, but anxious to avoid war, Nasser invited leaders of all the Arab states to a conference in Cairo. At the conference, Nasser argued that Israel's plans to divert the sources of the River Jordan was a threat to all Arab states.

The conference resulted in three significant developments.
1. The Headwater Diversion Plan was agreed on. Using Egyptian and Saudi money, Syria and Lebanon would divert two of the three sources of the River Jordan to prevent them from flowing into the Sea of Galilee. The aim was to stop Israel channelling fresh water from these sources to new settlements and farms in the dry south-west. If that did not succeed, then all Arab states would prepare for war in order to destroy Israel.
2. Arab support for Palestinians was made clear. The conference set up the Palestinian Liberation Organisation (PLO), to unite and lead all Palestinians in the struggle to regain their lost land. It was to be responsible for the welfare of Palestinians in refugee camps in Syria, Lebanon and Jordan. The PLO also to set up a Palestinian Liberation Army (PLA), so that Palestinians could join an army of their own.
3. As he had hoped, Nasser's leadership of the Arab world was confirmed. He had also proved he was clearly anti-Israeli without having to go to war.

THE IMPACT OF THE CAIRO CONFERENCE ON ISRAEL
Israel did not feel immediately threatened by the developments in Cairo. The Egyptian and Syrian armies were poorly trained and no match for the IDF, and

TENSION AND CONFLICT — MIDDLE EAST

Israel was buying modern military equipment from France and the USA. There were also UN peacekeeping troops in Sinai, which prevented any attacks on Israel from Egypt and Gaza. Israel was not worried about the setting up of the PLO or the PLA. At most, the PLA only ever had 12,000 soldiers.

However, the Headwater Diversion Plan was a different matter. When Syria started to construct a canal in 1965 to divert the flow of water away from Israel, Israel was concerned, so it prevented the canal's development by carrying out airstrikes in Syrian territory in April 1967 (see page 47). This dispute over water would become one of the causes of the Six Day War.

TENSION GROWS BETWEEN ISRAEL, SYRIA AND JORDAN

EXTEND YOUR KNOWLEDGE

YASSER ARAFAT
Yasser Arafat was born in Cairo in 1929. His father was a wealthy Palestinian merchant. As a young man, Arafat fought against Israel in the 1948–49 war and studied for an engineering degree in Cairo. He was expelled from Egypt following the Suez Crisis, and moved to Kuwait, where he founded Fatah. In 1962, he moved to Syria and, from 1965, Fatah developed into the largest Palestinian guerrilla force attacking Israel. As Chairman (head) of the PLO from 1969, Arafat was to become the best-known spokesman for the Palestinian cause.

SOURCE A
A photograph of Yasser Arafat in 1968. He is wearing a black and white *keffiyeh* on his head, which became a symbol of Palestinian nationalism.

FATAH
The Cairo Conference and the setting up of the PLO and the PLA made no real difference to most Palestinians. One group rejected the PLO completely: Fatah. Fatah, which means 'conquest' or 'victory', had been founded in 1959 by Yasser Arafat. He believed that the state of Israel had no right to exist and should be replaced by one state, Palestine, in which Jews and Arabs lived together. Arafat also believed that Palestinians had to stop waiting for the Arab states to solve their problems. He felt that only an armed struggle by Palestinians would destroy Israel, and he was prepared to use violent tactics to achieve this. He considered himself a freedom fighter; Israelis considered him a terrorist.

Arafat faced a problem: his group was small and unknown. It was one of many Palestinian **guerrilla** groups and many of his fighters were leaving to join the PLA. He decided that a big gesture was needed to win back support. On 1 January 1965, Fatah fighters slipped into Israel and laid explosives to destroy the canal that took fresh water from the Sea of Galilee to farms in the arid south-west. The mission failed: the bomb was discovered and defused by the Israelis. But then Arafat had a stroke of luck: the Israelis gave the plot huge publicity as evidence of the terrorism they faced. Suddenly Arafat was famous: he was a hero in the eyes of many Palestinians, and thousands joined Fatah.

SYRIAN SUPPORT FOR FATAH
Operating from bases in Jordan, Lebanon and Syria, Fatah launched over 100 raids on Israel in 1965–67. They laid explosives and land mines on roads, railway lines and water pipes, and they attacked villages. None of this would have been possible without Syrian support. Syria provided the funds, weapons and explosives. It also set up training camps for Fatah guerrillas inside Syria.

In February 1966, a new Syrian government seized power and increased support for Fatah. It also accused Nasser of doing nothing to help Palestinians. Nasser was hurt by this accusation. It was not his fault that Fatah could not operate out of Gaza. UN peacekeeping troops had been based there since the Suez Crisis and prevented raids into Israel. However, Nasser did agree to sign a defence pact with Syria: if either state was attacked by Israel, the other would come to its aid.

On the one hand, the Fatah raids were a failure: they did not destroy Israel (though 11 Israelis were killed and 62 wounded) and Israel retaliated every time. Because Israeli reprisals meant attacking Fatah targets inside Jordan and Lebanon, neither of these countries supported Arafat's tactics.

However, Arafat's popularity among Palestinians grew, and the raids kept the Palestinian cause in the news.

ISRAEL'S RAID ON SAMU, 13 NOVEMBER 1966

On 11 November 1966, an Israeli border patrol drove over a land mine near the Israeli–Jordanian border. Three Israeli policemen were killed and another six were wounded. Who laid the mine was unknown, but Fatah was suspected. Hoping to prevent a retaliation, King Hussein of Jordan wrote a letter of condolence to the Israeli prime minister, Levi Eshkol, (who had taken over from David Ben-Gurion in 1963) but it arrived too late.

On 13 November, Israel sent 600 troops, 11 tanks and 60 military vehicles into the West Bank. Their target was the small Arab settlement of Samu. There they ordered everyone to gather in the central square and then started to dynamite their homes. The whole operation was meant to be a quick raid but, by coincidence, about 100 Jordanian soldiers came across what was happening. In the battle that followed, 15 Jordanians, one Israeli and three villagers were killed; a Jordanian plane was shot down; and Samu was reduced to ruins.

THE CONSEQUENCES OF THE SAMU INCIDENT

The Samu Incident had serious consequences. Eshkol was strongly criticised, even at home, for sending such a large force and the attack was condemned by the UN. The USA was furious: Jordan was their only Arab ally in the region, and the only country that had been trying to establish good relations with Israel. Now Eshkol had wrecked that hope for peace.

The criticism Eshkol received made him cautious about further military action, but that meant that both Israelis and Arabs thought he was weak.

SOURCE B

The Jordanian border village of Samu, after being devastated by an IDF raid in November 1966.

The impact of the Samu Incident was even more serious for King Hussein. It almost destroyed him. He faced a storm of protest at home for failing to protect Palestinians and there were riots throughout the West Bank calling for his removal. To defend his position, the king abandoned his efforts to build good relations with Israel. He publicly called for revenge. However, Hussein did not want a war – he could not afford it. He also could not afford further Israeli retaliations, so he did his best to stop Fatah activity out of the West Bank.

However, saying one thing and then doing another meant that no one believed Hussein was seriously anti-Israeli. To defend his reputation with other Arab leaders, Hussein targeted Nasser. He accused Nasser of cowardice for not acting against Israel and of hiding behind the UN peacekeeping troops in Sinai. It was a clever accusation. It took the spotlight off Hussein and put Nasser under pressure to do something dramatic.

THE DOGFIGHT OF 7 APRIL 1967

Five months later, another incident raised the level of tension to a new high. This time the incident involved Syria and Israel, and it was about some fertile land by the Sea of Galilee. Since 1949, this land had been a UN-controlled **demilitarised zone (DMZ)**; it was overlooked by Syrian troops based high above it on the Golan Heights.

> **KEY TERMS**
>
> **DMZ (demilitarised zone)** an area where all military action is forbidden
>
> **dogfight** a close-range battle between military aircraft

On 7 April 1967, some Syrian gunners based in the Golan Heights fired on an Israeli tractor in the DMZ. In retaliation, the Israelis sent aeroplanes in to attack the Syrian gun positions. When Israeli aeroplanes also hit several Syrian villages up on the Golan Heights, the Syrians sent in their own fighter jets. A **dogfight** followed in which the Israelis shot down six Syrian jets and chased the rest back to Damascus. The loss of six jets in one day was a real blow to Syrian pride.

TENSION GROWS: THE ACTIONS OF THE USSR AND NASSER

Relations between Syria and Israel reached an all-time low by early May 1967. Israel demanded that Syria stop supporting the Fatah raids, which had increased in number.

On 13 May, the USSR got involved. It told Nasser that Israel was massing its troops on the Syrian border and about to attack Syria. This was completely untrue. The USSR may have been genuinely mistaken, or it may have been deliberately lying. No one knows. However, this false report put Nasser under huge pressure to do something. After all, Egypt and Syria had a defence pact. He was also meant to be the leader of the Arab world, but Syria and Jordan had now both accused him of hiding behind the UN and doing nothing to help Palestinians.

Nasser decided on some actions to show the Arabs that he was still a strong leader, and to make Israel think twice about attacking Syria. He began a fierce anti-Israeli **propaganda** campaign.

Nasser may have believed that Israel would give in to his demands (see 29 May in Figure 3.1) because, ever since the Samu Incident, Eshkol had seemed a weak leader. Perhaps Nasser also believed his own propaganda: that, if it came to war, the Arabs would win. After all, the Arab armies vastly outnumbered Israel's.

48 TENSION AND CONFLICT   THE MIDDLE EAST, 1917–2012

▼ Figure 3.1 Nasser increases the tension with Israel

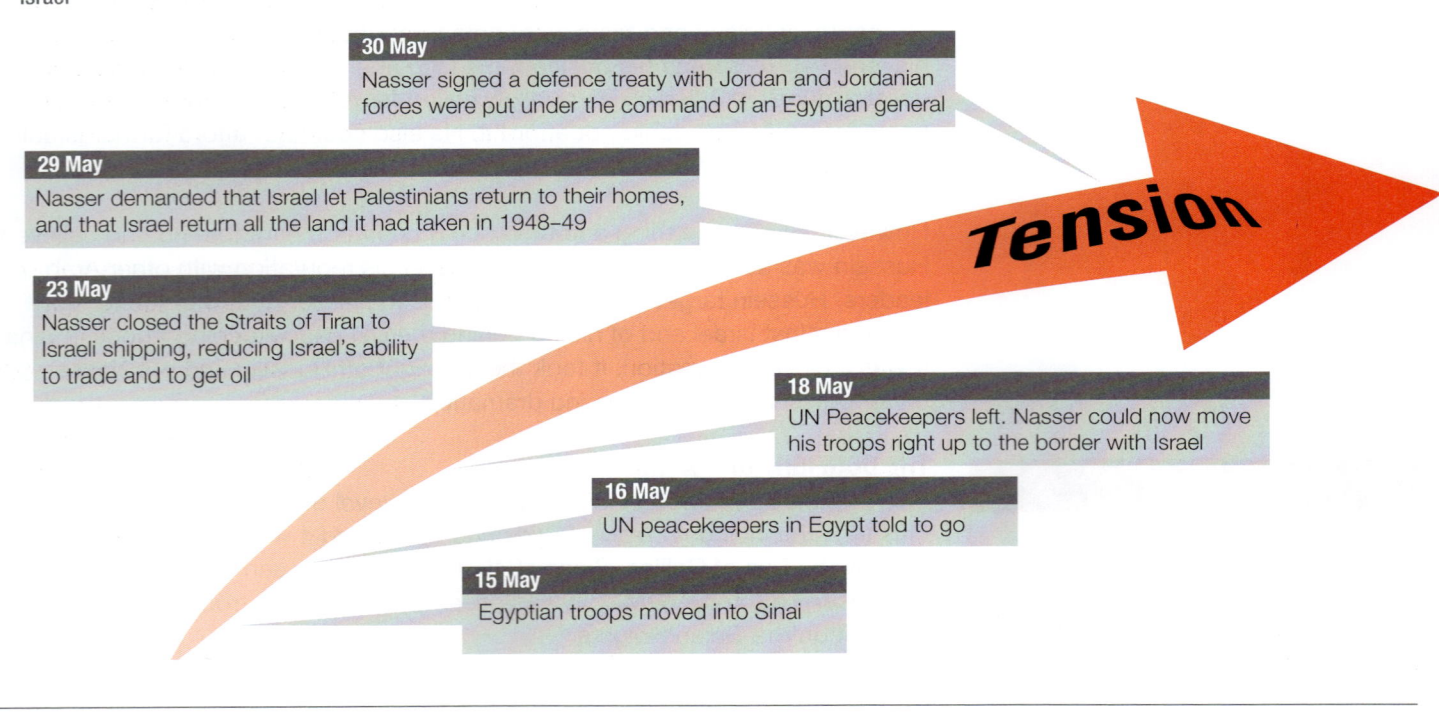

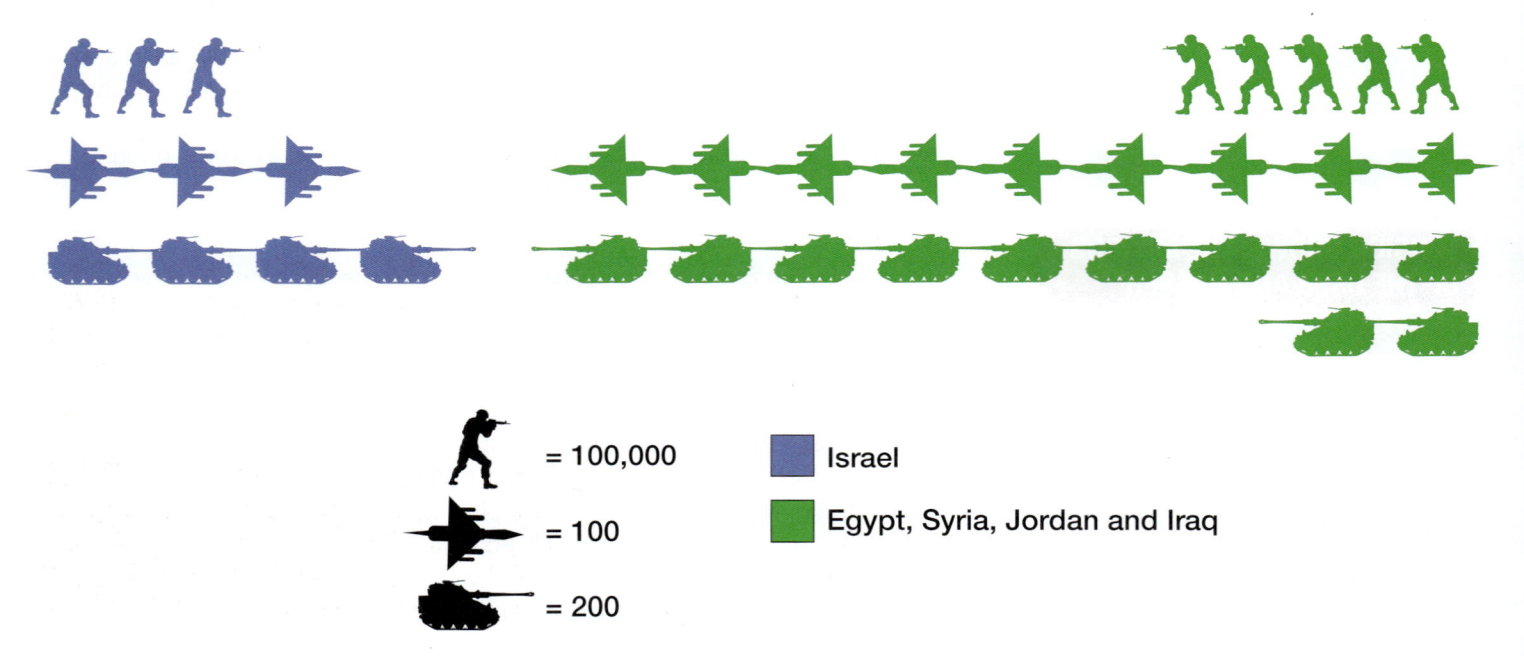

30 May
Nasser signed a defence treaty with Jordan and Jordanian forces were put under the command of an Egyptian general

29 May
Nasser demanded that Israel let Palestinians return to their homes, and that Israel return all the land it had taken in 1948–49

23 May
Nasser closed the Straits of Tiran to Israeli shipping, reducing Israel's ability to trade and to get oil

18 May
UN Peacekeepers left. Nasser could now move his troops right up to the border with Israel

16 May
UN peacekeepers in Egypt told to go

15 May
Egyptian troops moved into Sinai

Tension →

Key:
- 🧍 = 100,000
- ✈ = 100
- 🛡 (tank) = 200
- 🟦 Israel
- 🟩 Egypt, Syria, Jordan and Iraq

▲ Figure 3.2 The strength of each side in 1967

Nasser's actions meant that he was once again the hero of the Arabs. His actions convinced the public – everywhere – that Syria, Egypt and Jordan were about to launch a joint attack with the aim of destroying Israel, unless Israel complied with Nasser's demands.

TENSION AND CONFLICT **THE MIDDLE EAST, 1917–2012**

ISRAEL AND THE USA

The impact of Nasser's actions on Eshkol, though, was the opposite of what Nasser had hoped. Eshkol was not bullied into submission and he did not give way to Nasser's demands. He put Israel on military alert and called up the reserve troops. Weddings were postponed; people queued to donate blood; air raid shelters were dug; parks were consecrated (blessed) for possible use as mass cemeteries. Emergency appeals were issued to Jews worldwide to help by donating money; some even flew to Israel to lend their support. The tension became unbearable.

Eshkol did not want to make the first move, but the Straits of Tiran had to be reopened (see Figure 3.1). He hoped that the USA would intervene, but they refused. Then, on 31 May, the USA suggested that Israel take action itself to open the Straits. It was not exactly what Eshkol had wanted, but at least Israel had US support to act. The following day, Eshkol appointed Moshe Dayan as Defence Minister. Dayan believed that, if Israel launched a surprise attack immediately, it would easily be able to defeat the Arab armies and reopen the Straits of Tiran. Dayan did not want to alert the enemy, so he announced that reserve troops could go home for the weekend. On 4 June, in top secret, the Israeli government decided on war.

ACTIVITY

1 Draw a timeline to cover the period January 1965 to June 1967. Add 6–10 events to your timeline.
2 Choose any two of these events and explain how they link together. Then do this for two more pairs of events.
3 Which event do you think resulted in the most tension? Why do you think that?

3.2 THE SIX DAY WAR

LEARNING OBJECTIVES

- Understand the key events of the Six Day War, 1967
- Understand the reasons for Israel's success
- Understand the impact of the Six Day War on Israel and on the Arab states, especially Egypt.

Without warning, Israel launched its attack on 5 June 1967. At dawn, almost the entire Israeli air force set off for Egypt. By 11 a.m. it had destroyed 309 Egyptian aircraft (out of a total of 340) and bombed all 19 of Egypt's airfields. The Israeli air force then turned to target the airfields of Syria and Jordan. By nightfall, Israel controlled the skies and its land forces could attack. IDF tanks moved quickly across Sinai, destroying Egyptian tanks as they went. By 7 June, Israeli forces had reached the Suez Canal.

TENSION AND CONFLICT — THE MIDDLE EAST, 1917–2012

SOURCE C

Israeli soldiers celebrate victory at the end of the Six Day War.

Meanwhile, Israel was fighting Jordanian troops in Jerusalem and, on 7 June, the IDF won control of East Jerusalem. On 8 June, ignoring Jordan's request for a ceasefire, the IDF took control of the West Bank. Only then did the IDF turn its attention north. By 9 June, the Golan Heights had been captured and IDF forces had moved nearly 50 km into Syria itself.

▼ Figure 3.3 A timeline of the fighting in the Six Day War

1967	Israel v. Egypt	Israel v. Syria	Israel v. Jordan
5 June	IDF destroy Egypt's air forces and airfields. IDF occupy the Gaza Strip.	IDF destroy Syria's air forces and airfields.	IDF destroy Jordan's air forces and airfields. Jordanian forces attack west Jerusalem.
6 June	IDF tanks cross Sinai towards the Suez Canal.		Fierce fighting for control of Jerusalem.
7 June	IDF achieve complete control of Sinai.		IDF win control of east Jerusalem. Jordan accepts UN call for a ceasefire.
8 June	Egypt accepts UN call for a ceasefire.		IDF take complete control of the West Bank.
9 June		IDF attack the Syrian army in the Golan Heights.	
10 June		IDF take complete control of the Golan Heights. Syria accepts UN call for a ceasefire.	

ISRAELI GAINS

KEY TERM

pre-emptive strike a surprise attack based on the belief that the enemy is about to attack you and that the only way to defend yourself is to attack first

▶ Figure 3.4 Reasons for Israel's success in 1967

In just 6 days, Israel achieved a spectacular victory. While 779 Israelis were killed, Arab losses were staggering: about 20,000 men were killed, 430 aircraft and 800 tanks had been destroyed, and 70,000 square kilometres of land had been taken. Given the aggressive actions of the Arabs before the war, Israel's attack on 5 June was effectively a **pre-emptive strike**, to prevent Israel from coming under attack.

Tactics
- use of surprise
- ensuring control of the air first
- then tackling one enemy at a time

The IDF
- very well-trained and highly motivated air force and army
- superior tanks and weapons

Arab weaknesses
- unprepared
- poorly trained and equipped troops
- poorly co-ordinated: they all agreed to truces at different times

TENSION AND CONFLICT — THE MIDDLE EAST, 1917–2012

EXTEND YOUR KNOWLEDGE

AN ALTERNATIVE INTERPRETATION: EGYPT'S POINT OF VIEW

According to this point of view, Moshe Dayan knew that Nasser's actions were taken only to save face, and the Israelis also knew that Egypt and Syria would be easy to defeat in a war. However, Israel wanted to take more land, and Nasser's closure of the Straits of Tiran provided an excuse. So Israel presented itself as acting in self-defence in June 1967, but actually acted aggressively and illegally. For example, it refused Jordan's offer of a ceasefire until it had control of the West Bank and East Jerusalem. Even the USA was taken in: it had agreed to Israeli action to reopen the Straits of Tiran but it did not know about Israel's intention to take so much land. That might explain why a US spy ship in the Mediterranean, the USS *Liberty*, was attacked by the Israelis: to prevent the US learning about Israel's ambition to take control of the Golan Heights.

After the war, Nasser defended some of his aggressive actions, like ordering UN peacekeepers out of Sinai and moving troops up to the border, by saying that he had just hoped this would act as a warning to Israel not to invade Syria. He also said that he did not actually expect the UN to leave Sinai; he thought the UN would refuse to go.

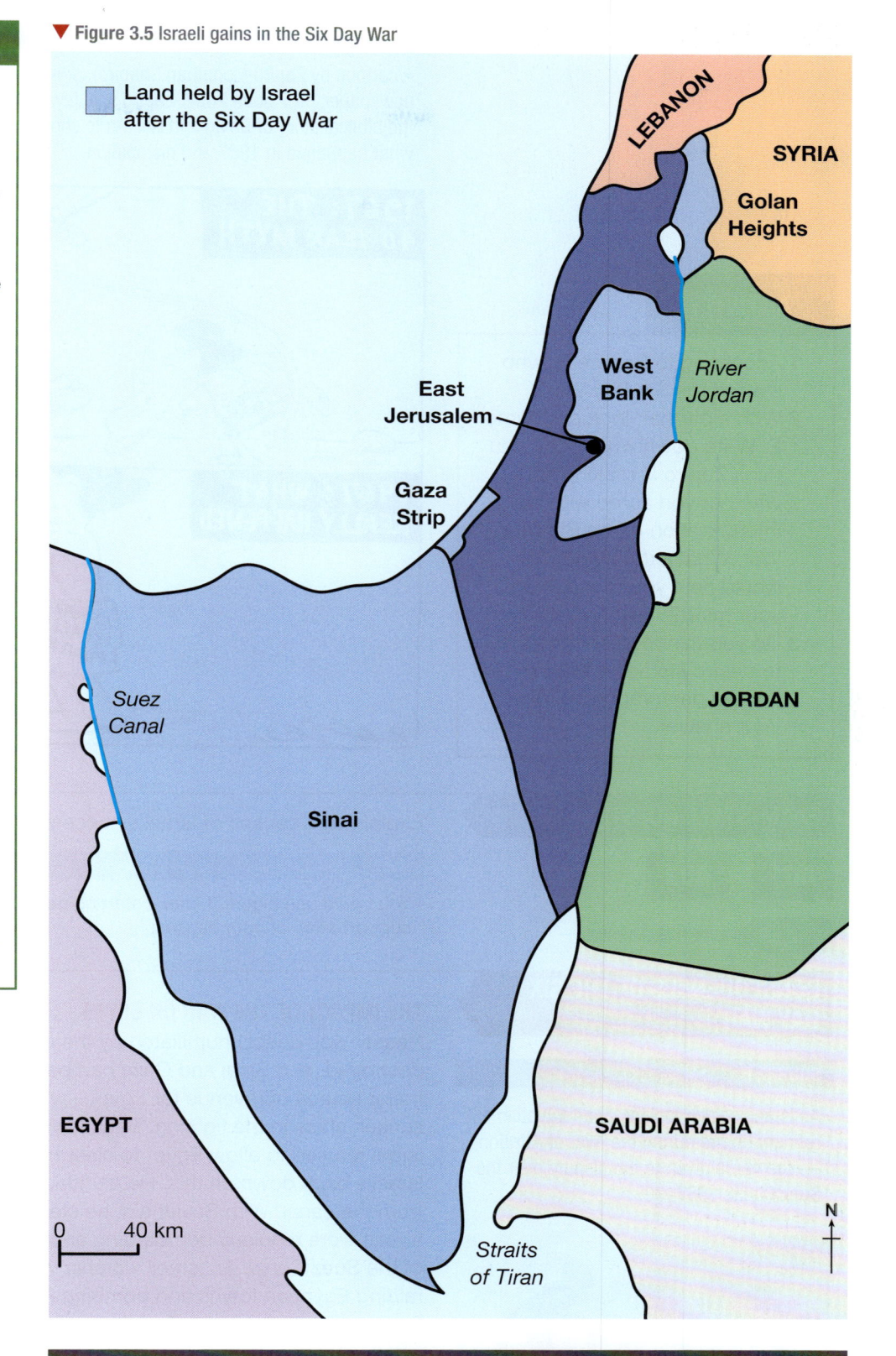

▼ Figure 3.5 Israeli gains in the Six Day War

SOURCE D

From an article written in 1992 by an American journalist.

Today what is clear is that the Israelis wanted war, Egypt did not, the Soviets could have prevented it, and the Americans should have.

SOURCE E

A cartoon by Zapiro (Jonathan Shapiro), printed in *Mail and Guardian*, a South African newspaper, on 7 June 2007. Zapiro is a Jewish South African cartoonist and here he uses the biblical story of David and Goliath to show the difference between the popular theory of what happened in 1967 and his opinion.

ACTIVITY

1. According to Source D, who started the Six Day War?
2. With a partner, look at Source E. Write down what point you think Zapiro is making and whether you agree with his interpretation of the Six Day War. What extra evidence would help you to make up your mind?
3. Do you think Nasser intended to destroy Israel in 1967? Write a paragraph to explain your answer.

EXAM-STYLE QUESTION

AO1 **AO2**

SKILLS ADAPTIVE LEARNING

Explain **two** causes of Israel's success in the Six Day War (1967). **(8 marks)**

HINT

You could use Figure 3.4 as a starting point. You will need to provide details to support each of your causes.

CONSEQUENCES OF THE SIX DAY WAR

SOURCE F

An Israeli soldier looking at an Egyptian oil refinery on fire during the 'War of Attrition' — the name given to the dispute over the Suez Canal, 1967–70.

THE IMPACT OF THE WAR ON EGYPT

Nasser was deeply humiliated by the defeat of 1967. Egyptian forces had been destroyed, and Sinai and Gaza had been taken. Crucially, the Suez Canal – a major source of revenue for Egypt – was unusable as it had been blocked by sunken ships in the fighting. Because Egypt refused to let Israel use the canal, Israel refused to allow Egypt to clear these ships. Nasser needed to make the Israelis back down on this. He decided to try and force them to move away from the canal. With Soviet aid, he started rearming and, within a year, Egyptian forces were regularly bombarding and raiding Israeli positions on the Sinai side of the Suez Canal. An Israeli warship was sunk. The Israelis retaliated fiercely, raiding Egyptian towns and bombing Egyptian cities and oil refineries (see Source F), which badly affected the Egyptian economy.

By 1970, this '**War of Attrition**' (as Nasser called it) over the Suez Canal had escalated dangerously. Over 1.5 million Egyptians had fled their homes, while about 1,000 Israelis had been killed. Worse still, both sides were calling in superpower aid. The USSR provided Egypt with 100 fighter planes and also gave them SAM-3 (surface-to-air) anti-aircraft missiles to defend the

Aswan Dam, while 20,000 Soviet troops arrived to build 80 missile bases. The SAM-3 missiles meant that Israel's air force could no longer fly over Egyptian soil. The USA supported Israel with weapons and aid, and became increasingly concerned that events could lead to an East versus West confrontation. So it organised a ceasefire in August 1970. Both sides realised no one could win the War of Attrition and accepted the ceasefire. But this was only a short-term solution to the tension.

THE IMPACT OF THE WAR ON ISRAEL

The Six Day War was a massive victory for Israel. It had won a victory against the odds and it had captured East Jerusalem, which contained the Wailing Wall and Temple Mount (the two holiest sites for the Jews), the West Bank, the Gaza Strip, Sinai and the Golan Heights. It was now 350 per cent bigger. Huge amounts of captured Soviet weapons were now in Israeli hands, while the forces of Israel's enemies had been utterly destroyed. Morale had never been higher.

Israelis were divided about what to do with the land that they had conquered in the Six Day War, as Figure 3.6 shows.

SOURCE G

An Israeli photographer remembers how victory felt in 1967.

We went from being doomed to having an empire. It was like a condemned man with a noose around his neck suddenly being told that not only was he going to live but he was going to be king.

▶ Figure 3.6 Different views on what Israel should do with the land it had captured

Give it back
- Taking land is illegal. It must be returned or it will cause endless problems.
- Land for Peace is the way forward. The land can be restored to its rightful owner in return for peace.

Keep it
- Israel has a growing population and needs the extra land and resources.
- The territories provide greater security. Israel has more control over its borders.
- Jerusalem has great religious importance. The captured land means that Israel controls all of the Promised Land given by God.

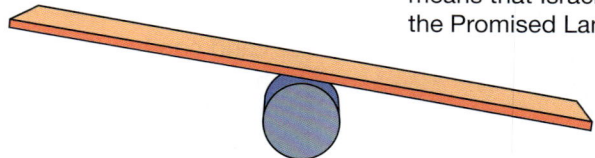

There were several other factors to be considered.
- International law states that a country cannot annex or indefinitely occupy territory gained by force, nor can it bring its own people to live in an occupied territory. Global public opinion would turn against Israel if it kept its territorial gains.
- Annexing the occupied territories – making them a full part of Israel – would mean making 1 million Arabs into Israeli citizens and giving them the vote. They would almost outnumber the Jews.
- Military occupation would be expensive and would be resented (and resisted) by Palestinians, as well as causing international criticism.

The table below summarises the significance of the territories Israel gained to both Israel and the Arabs.

OCCUPIED TERRITORY	SIGNIFICANCE TO ISRAEL	SIGNIFICANCE TO ARABS
East Jerusalem	The Wailing Wall and Temple Mount are the holiest sites for Jews.	The Dome of the Rock and the Al-Aqsa Mosque are holy sites for Muslims.
West Bank	Gives Israel a buffer zone between itself and Jordan. Israel has a growing population and needs the fertile land beside the River Jordan. Part of the Promised Land given to Jews by God.	The West Bank is home to over 600,000 Palestinians. Jewish settlement here is very unpopular. Jordan had annexed the West Bank – they believed it belonged to them.
Gaza	Israel can clamp down on the Fedayeen raids from the refugee camps in Gaza.	Gaza is home to 350,000 people, mostly Palestinians, who resent Israeli interference in their lives. Egypt had occupied Gaza since 1948, but allowed Palestinians some self-government there.
Sinai	Gives Israel a buffer zone between itself and Egypt. Trade through the Straits of Tiran is now safe, and Sinai's oil reserves are useful.	Sinai legally belongs to Egypt. It contains Egypt's only oil supplies. Israeli occupation prevents use of the Suez Canal. Its tolls are essential to Egypt's economy.
Golan Heights	Syria is no longer able to fire on Israeli farms in Galilee. Golan's fertile land and fresh water sources are invaluable.	Israel can fire on Syrian towns, including Damascus. The Golan Heights had been home to about 100,000 Syrians. Golan's fertile land and water sources are important for Syria.

ACTIVITY

Land can be significant for many different reasons. For example, it can have religious, political, economic or military significance.
1. Explain the significance of East Jerusalem to Jews.
2. Look at each of the other occupied territories captured by Israel and explain its significance to Israelis. Use the table above to help you.
3. Explain the significance of the occupied territories, including Jerusalem, to Egypt, Syria, Jordan and the Palestinians. Use the table above to help you.
4. What do you think of the views in Figure 3.6? What would you have done?

SOURCE H

Israeli soldiers pray at the Wailing Wall, June 1967.

A mixture of the policies shown in Figure 3.6 were followed. However, the extreme left view (that the land should be returned) was ignored as the Israeli Communist Party did not have much influence in the Knesset.

Almost everyone agreed on one point: what to do with East Jerusalem. It contained the Old City, with the Wailing Wall and Temple Mount, and Israelis were determined that it should stay in Jewish hands forever. It was going to be annexed.

The rest of the captured land was put under military control and became known as the occupied territories. Controlling Gaza meant Israel could clamp down on the Fedayeen raids that had come from there. Controlling the West Bank, the Golan Heights and Sinai meant that Israel now had the security of

TENSION AND CONFLICT — THE MIDDLE EAST, 1917–2012

KEY TERM

buffer zone a peaceful area between two countries created to prevent conflict between them

a **buffer zone** between itself and Jordan, Syria and Egypt. Trade through the Gulf of Aqaba would be safe, and Golan's fertile land and water, and Sinai's oil reserves, would be useful. However, the 'War of Attrition' over the Suez Canal zone was very expensive. Privately, some Israelis thought that Sinai should be returned to Egyptian hands in return for a lasting peace agreement. Not everyone agreed with this view though. Many Israelis, including Golda Meir (prime minister from 1969), thought that Egypt could never be trusted.

UN RESOLUTION 242

Six months after the Six Day War had ended, the United Nations adopted Resolution 242. It attempted to settle the Arab–Israeli conflict with a 'Land for Peace' solution, and both the USA and the USSR voted in favour of it. Resolution 242 stated:

- Israel must withdraw from 'territories occupied in the recent conflict'
- in return, Arab states must recognise Israel's right to exist
- there should be a 'just settlement of the refugee problem'.

Resolution 242 had a mixed reception. Palestinians rejected it: the reference to them as a 'refugee problem' was insulting and the 'Land for Peace' idea ignored Palestinian land claims that dated back to 1948–49. Israel said it was prepared to negotiate, separately, with Egypt, Jordan and Syria over the territories it occupied, but did not commit to fully withdrawing from them.

Egypt and Jordan initially agreed with Resolution 242, but this changed when the Arab states met at a conference in Khartoum in August 1967. At the conference, the Arab states, including Egypt, Jordan and Syria, publicly rejected Israel's right to exist and responded with what became known as the 'Three Nos': no peace with Israel, no recognition of Israel, no negotiations with Israel. Nasser said he would accept Resolution 242, but Israel had to pull out of all the territories it had occupied first. Until then he followed the 'Three Nos' and that meant no peace.

3.3 PALESTINIAN RESISTANCE

LEARNING OBJECTIVES

- Understand the reasons for the growth of Palestinian guerrilla groups
- Understand the divisions in the Palestinian resistance movement
- Understand the impact of Palestinian terrorism.

THE PLIGHT OF THE PALESTINIANS

The Six Day War was a disaster for Palestinians. The 1 million Palestinians who lived in the West Bank and Gaza found themselves under Israeli military control. Many of those who had lived in and around East Jerusalem were evicted and forced to live elsewhere in the West Bank.

About 300,000 Palestinians had chosen not to stay in the West Bank when it was captured by the Israelis. Most fled to Jordan, where six new emergency refugee camps were set up by the UN. Life in these refugee camps was very basic. Baqa'a, the largest, had 26,000 refugees living in 5,000 tents in an area of 1.4 square km. Though the tents were eventually replaced with prefabricated structures, life was grim. Along with poverty and high unemployment, the camps lacked facilities and services like rubbish collection.

With a few exceptions, these Palestinian refugees were not allowed to become citizens in the Arab countries where they now lived. This meant they could not vote and did not receive passports, which made travel difficult. The sort of work they could do was also restricted. Refugees living in Lebanon, for example, were not allowed to work as lawyers, doctors and engineers. The view of the Arab states was that, since these refugees had been displaced by Israel, they should be rehomed and compensated by Israel. This explains why Arab states refused to absorb the Palestinians into their own countries, but instead insisted that they remain refugees. Israel's view was that, since about 850,000 Jews had moved from Arab states into Israel (see pages 30–32), Arab states should take responsibility for the Palestinians.

Unsurprisingly, many of these Palestinian refugees joined guerrilla movements, determined to fight to recover the land they had lost. Most put their faith in Yasser Arafat's Fatah. He moved Fatah's headquarters to Jordan after the Six Day War.

PALESTINIAN ACTIVISM AND THE USE OF TERRORISM

From 1948 to 1967, Palestinians hoped that neighbouring Arab states would destroy Israel. But the complete defeat of Egypt, Syria and Jordan in the Six Day War made it clear to Palestinians that they could only rely on themselves to win back their homeland.

> **SOURCE I**
>
> Extract from an interview with a Palestinian refugee in 2007.
>
> It was a time of optimism before the war [Six Day War]. We were all fascinated by Nasser and we believed if the Arabs were united they could defeat anyone. We were glued to the radio in the dormitories and the cafeteria and were happy when we heard that the Israeli air force had been destroyed. It meant that all of us from Jaffa, Jerusalem or the Galilee could go home.
>
> Slowly the truth began to emerge. We could not believe that the Egyptians had been so weak after their years of bragging. We cried like children. We were lost; we were outside our homes and we had nowhere to go. My friends and I began to feel that the defeat was as much about the betrayal by the Arab leaders as it was about the strength of Israel.

However, the Palestinian resistance movement was divided. Although all wanted the destruction of Israel and the recovery of their homeland, over 30 Fedayeen groups operated from Jordan alone and they did not co-ordinate their actions. There were two main ideas about which tactics to use.

- Arafat's group, Fatah, continued to launch guerrilla attacks on Israel from its bases in Jordan and Lebanon: they aimed to force Israel to leave the occupied territories.
- Newer groups, like the Popular Front for the Liberation of Palestine (**PFLP**), believed that terrorist action outside of Israel was the key. This would draw global attention to the Palestinians and force foreign governments to do something about the problem.

KEY TERM

PFLP Palestinian guerrilla group formed in 1967. It was founded by a Palestinian Christian called Dr George Habash. As a young man, he was among thousands of Arabs expelled from Lydda (see page 26) by Israeli troops. Habash was a Communist and in the 1970s the PFLP was partly funded by communist countries like China and the USSR

TENSION AND CONFLICT — THE MIDDLE EAST, 1917–2012

FATAH GUERRILLA ATTACKS

Fatah was able to recruit many new members after the Six Day War. It was also better armed, since it was able to use the weapons abandoned by Arab armies during the war. From his new headquarters in Karameh, in Jordan, Arafat ordered waves of attacks on Israel. Israel always retaliated. The crisis peaked when a Fatah mine blew up an Israeli school bus in March 1968, killing the teachers and wounding ten children. It was the 38th Fatah operation that year and Israel decided to destroy Karameh, even though that meant crossing into Jordan. It sent in 15,000 troops, but these faced strong resistance from the Fatah guerrillas, who were supported by Jordanian troops, something Israel had not expected. What started as a raid turned into a 15-hour long battle.

In one sense Israel won. It destroyed Fatah's base in Karameh and took 150 prisoners. However, it lost 28 soldiers, 27 tanks and two aircraft. It was also condemned by world opinion for its use of excessive force. The battle at Karameh backfired in another way: Fatah's strength grew. 5,000 new recruits joined within 2 days of the battle and, in 1969 alone, there were over 2,000 Fatah attacks on Israel. Meanwhile, Yasser Arafat's reputation as a strong leader was boosted so much that, in 1969, he was made the Chairman of the PLO.

ACTIVITY

'The Israeli attack on Karameh destroyed the Fatah base there, so it was a complete success.' Do you agree?

PFLP AEROPLANE HIJACKS: DAWSON'S FIELD, 1970

SOURCE J

Dr George Habash, leader of the PFLP, explains the purpose of hijacking aeroplanes in a German magazine in 1970.

When we hijack a plane it has more effect than if we killed a hundred Israelis in battle. For decades world public opinion has been neither for nor against the Palestinians. It has simply ignored us. At least the world is now talking about us.

From the PFLP's point of view, Fatah tactics achieved nothing. Any attack on an Israeli target, wherever it happened, led to massive retaliation, which usually meant bombing Fatah bases in Lebanon, Jordan or Syria. Since these were near Palestinian refugee camps, many innocent Palestinian civilians died. Instead, George Habash organised the **hijacking** of aeroplanes.

In September 1970, Habash masterminded his most famous action. The PFLP hijacked four aeroplanes and flew three of them to Dawson's Field, a remote desert airstrip in Jordan. The 310 passengers were allowed to disembark. Most were released, but 56 Jews were separated out, to be kept as hostages until Israel freed four PFLP prisoners (which they eventually did). Then, as the invited world's press watched, the PFLP blew up the planes (see Source K).

SOURCE K

The PFLP blows up aeroplanes on Dawson's Field, September 1970.

BLACK SEPTEMBER AND THE EXPULSION OF THE PLO FROM JORDAN

By 1970, over half of the population of Jordan were Palestinian refugees. Most saw Yasser Arafat, now Chairman of the PLO, as their leader. As a result, Arafat and his 20,000 Fatah fighters in Jordan effectively controlled a state-within-a-state that challenged King Hussein's position as ruler of Jordan. It was even rumoured that the PLO planned to overthrow King Hussein. The PLO also used Jordan as a base for its operations against Israel. These operations angered King Hussein since the Israelis always retaliated, causing damage to Jordan. Even before Dawson's Field, therefore, tension between the PLO and King Hussein had reached breaking point.

King Hussein of Jordan was furious about the aeroplane hijackings. He felt that the Palestinian groups were abusing his hospitality (the PFLP were also based in Jordan at this time). The fact that the aeroplanes were British, Swiss and American also meant that foreign intervention was a strong possibility unless he acted. He ordered his army to seize control of Palestinian bases, whatever the resistance. Over 10 days – known as 'Black September' to Palestinians – Jordanian troops killed nearly 2,000 Palestinian fighters. There was some respite when Nasser negotiated a truce, but hostilities resumed when Nasser suddenly died of a heart attack in 1970.

By July 1971, King Hussain was back in control of his country. He had expelled the PLO leadership and thousands of Palestinian fighters from Jordan. Most moved to Lebanon, and the PLO set up their new headquarters in Beirut, the capital.

ACTIVITY

1. Write one sentence to explain why you think the PFLP hijacked and then blew up aeroplanes in Dawson's Field.
2. King Hussein was an Arab; his country had declared war on Israel in 1948 and in 1967. With a partner, discuss the reasons why King Hussein declared war on the PLO in 1970 and expelled them from his country. Which reason do you think was most important?
3. Was the PFLP's Dawson's Field operation a success or a failure? Draw up a balance sheet of pluses and minuses to help you reach a judgement and then write a paragraph to explain the judgement you reached.

MASSACRE AT THE MUNICH OLYMPICS, 1972

In the aftermath of the PLO's expulsion from Jordan, an extreme group emerged. It called itself the Black September Organisation (a reference to the Jordanian attack on Palestinian fighters in 1970), and its first act was one of revenge: the assassination of the Jordanian prime minister. Its next target was the 1972 Olympic Games, which were held in Munich, Germany. At 4.30 a.m. on 5 September, eight armed members of Black September entered the Olympic Village and seized control of two apartments used by the Israeli team. Two Israeli athletes were shot dead; a further nine were taken hostage. Black September then demanded the immediate release by Israel of 234 Palestinian prisoners. German negotiators agreed to helicopter the terrorists and their hostages to a military airbase, from where they would be flown to an Arab country. But at the airport an attempt was made by West German police to free the hostages. In the gun battle that followed, all nine athletes and five of the terrorists were killed. The three surviving terrorists were taken prisoner.

ACTIVITY

Why do you think that the Black September Organisation targeted the Munich Olympics?

EXAM-STYLE QUESTION

AO1 AO2

Explain **two** ways in which Palestinian attacks on Israel in the 1970s were different from those of the 1960s. **(6 marks)**

HINT

Be sure to write about two ways. For each way, you will get one mark for identifying a difference (for example, a difference in tactics), another mark for explaining that difference, and a third mark for using supporting information.

TENSION AND CONFLICT — **THE MIDDLE EAST, 1917–2012**

THE IMPACT OF TERRORISM

The PFLP and the Black September Organisation wanted to raise international awareness of the Palestinian issue, and they succeeded. However, public opinion was outraged. Around the world there was a flood of sympathy for Israel after the events in Munich.

The activities of terrorist groups also failed to change Israeli policy. Following the attack in Munich, Israeli Prime Minister Golda Meir ordered air attacks on Syria and Lebanon, which killed approximately 200–500 people. She also launched Operation Wrath of God, which secretly authorised Mossad to find and assassinate all those responsible for the Munich massacre. She wanted revenge and she wanted to **deter** future attacks by making Palestinian terrorist leaders feel frightened.

But Operation Wrath of God failed as a deterrent. Terrorist incidents continued and Israel also received negative publicity when innocent bystanders were killed during Mossad operations. Meanwhile, those terrorists assassinated by Mossad became heroes in Palestinian eyes. For example, when one of the Black September masterminds behind the Munich attack, Ali Hassan Salameh, was assassinated in 1979, 20,000 (some say 100,000) Palestinians attended his funeral.

The terrorism and reprisals of the late 1960s and 1970s ensured that world attention was refocused on the problems in Palestine. A dispute over land in the Middle East was putting everyone at risk, and international pressure to find a solution slowly increased, even if this meant inviting a 'moderate' Palestinian like the Fatah leader, Yasser Arafat, to explain his view to the UN (see Chapter 4).

3.4 THE YOM KIPPUR WAR, 1973

LEARNING OBJECTIVES

- Understand why Egypt and Syria decided to attack Israel in 1973
- Understand the reasons for early Arab successes in the Yom Kippur War
- Understand the reasons for the eventual Israeli recovery
- Understand the effects of the Yom Kippur War on the Arab–Israeli conflict.

ANWAR SADAT

On 28 September 1970, just after he had negotiated a truce between the PLO and King Hussein of Jordan (see page 58), Nasser suffered a heart attack and died. Five million mourners attended his funeral in Cairo. Among them were King Hussein and Yasser Arafat, both of whom wept openly.

Anwar Sadat became the new president of Egypt. He was an unlikely candidate to be president: he lacked charisma and he was almost unknown outside Egypt. He also had to put up with racist jokes due to the fact that he was part Sudanese.

However, underestimating Sadat was a mistake. His main aim was to restore Egypt's economy and rebuild cities destroyed in the War of Attrition (see page 52). To do that he needed to cut military spending and send home the million soldiers on standby in case of an Israeli attack. He also needed to reopen the Suez Canal so that toll money could be collected. To do all these things, he needed peace with Israel, which meant that the return of Sinai had to come first. For 2 years, Sadat tried a variety of tactics.

- He approached Prime Minister Golda Meir with an offer based on Resolution 242: peace in return for Sinai. She rejected his offer.
- He expelled 15,000 Soviet military advisers, hoping this would please the USA and encourage them to put pressure on Israel to negotiate. The USA, however, did not do this.

By late 1972, Sadat's popularity in Egypt was at its lowest: the economy was still failing, the Canal was still closed, and Sinai was still in Israeli hands.

Frustrated, Sadat decided the only way to make Israel negotiate was to make it feel threatened. In secret, he started preparing for war. The plan was a simple one: Egypt and its ally, Syria, would launch a co-ordinated surprise attack on Israel. The goal was limited to making Israel realise that it was not invincible. Then it might agree to negotiate over Sinai and the Golan Heights.

ISRAELI CONTROL OF SINAI AND THE GOLAN HEIGHTS

While Sadat was trying to secure the return of Sinai by negotiation, Israel continued fortifying it. Golda Meir did not believe that Sadat genuinely wanted 'land for peace'. To prevent an Egyptian attack, a steep 20–25 m high wall of sand had been built along the length of the Suez Canal. Behind this a line of forts with deep bunkers were built, each surrounded by minefields and barbed wire. These defences were known as the Bar Lev Line and cost about $300 million to build. Defences were also built up in the Golan Heights, to prevent an attack there from Syria. Deep bunkers were dug and fortified with steel. The 100,000 Syrians who had fled from Golan during the Six Day War were not permitted to return.

Secure behind its occupied territories, Israel felt safe. An attack seemed unlikely: Egypt had expelled its Soviet advisers and it would surely take the Arabs years to rebuild their armed forces. Also, since the Munich massacre of 1972, world sympathy had been on Israel's side and US aid was pouring in.

EXAM-STYLE QUESTION

AO1 AO2

SKILLS ADAPTIVE LEARNING

Explain **two** causes of the Yom Kippur War (1973). **(8 marks)**

HINT
You will get a maximum of 4 marks if you only deal with one cause, so remember to deal with two.

WAR!

Yom Kippur is the holiest day of the year in Judaism. In 1973, Yom Kippur fell on Saturday, 6 October. Across Israel, buses and cars were parked up, businesses and shops were closed, and radios and televisions were silent. The streets were empty and **synagogues** were full. Many soldiers were home on leave, observing Yom Kippur with their families. Israel was totally unprepared for what was about to happen.

At 2 p.m. Egypt launched a surprise attack on Sinai. The Egyptian air force bombed Israeli airfields and army bases in Sinai while Egyptian **artillery** bombed the Bar Lev Line. About 10,500 shells were launched in the first

TENSION AND CONFLICT   THE MIDDLE EAST, 1917–2012

> ### EXTEND YOUR KNOWLEDGE
>
> #### WARNING SIGNS FOR ISRAEL
> Israel did ignore some warning signs. Egyptian and Syrian troops had been collecting on the borders for weeks, but they cleverly hid their intentions by pretending to withdraw every evening. During the day, Egyptian soldiers sunbathed by the Suez Canal, which was another clever way to lull Israel into a false sense of security.
>
> King Hussein of Jordan warned Israel about an attack. At 4.30 a.m. on 6 October, the Israeli chief of staff, General Eleazar, was even told by Mossad that an attack would happen 'in hours'. He wanted to strike Arab forces immediately, but Golda Meir refused. She said that Israel must appear as a victim, not as the aggressor. She may not have believed the report anyway since there had already been several false alarms.

SOURCE L

An Egyptian soldier celebrates the crossing of the Suez Canal, October 1973.

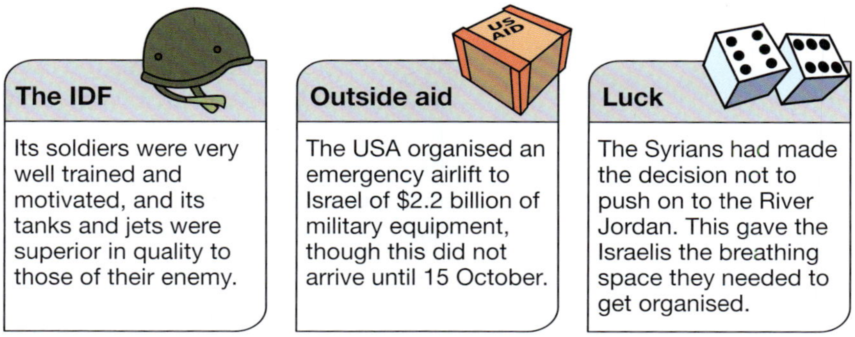

▶ Figure 3.7 The three things that saved Israel in 1973

minute alone. Getting more troops into Sinai depended on opening up passages through the high wall of sand. High pressure water cannons were taken over on wooden boats and, in 70 places, the sand wall was blasted with water from the Canal, creating the necessary passages. Egyptian engineers then built temporary bridges over the Canal and, by 4.30 p.m., 23,000 Egyptian troops had poured into Sinai. It was a remarkable achievement.

The Israelis were in for another surprise: the Egyptians were very well armed. IDF troops in the Bar Lev Line forts hoped the Israeli air force would come to their rescue, but the first Israeli jets were shot down by Soviet-built SAM-3 missiles. Israeli tanks racing towards the Canal to stop the invasion came under attack from Soviet-built Sagger anti-tank missiles. About half of the 300 IDF tanks present in Sinai were destroyed by the second day of the war.

At 2 p.m. (exactly the same time that Egypt attacked), Syrian forces invaded the Golan Heights. Israel was clearly not expecting an attack since it had only 170 tanks and 400 troops stationed there. Syria launched its attack using 1,200 tanks and 60,000 troops. Within 6 hours, Israeli defences to the south had been overrun. Syrian tanks raced past the Israeli bunkers towards the edge of Golan and threatened Israel's heartland.

Israel had been taken by surprise. The usual radio silence of Yom Kippur was lifted and every reserve soldier was ordered to report immediately for duty. Troops even had to be despatched on motorbikes to raise the alarm since so many families had their radios switched off or were at prayer in synagogues. At least the roads were clear because of Yom Kippur, which made moving troops easier. It still took Israel 72 hours to **mobilise** completely.

Why did the Arabs have early success in the war?
- The Israelis were not expecting an attack and thought that the Bev Line would protect them.
- It was Yom Kippur and Israeli soldiers were on leave.
- The Egyptians were better armed than the Israelis thought.
- The attack from Syria was a surprise.
- Israel ignored warnings from Jordan and Mossad.

Israel's survival was helped by three things:

The IDF	Outside aid	Luck
Its soldiers were very well trained and motivated, and its tanks and jets were superior in quality to those of their enemy.	The USA organised an emergency airlift to Israel of $2.2 billion of military equipment, though this did not arrive until 15 October.	The Syrians had made the decision not to push on to the River Jordan. This gave the Israelis the breathing space they needed to get organised.

Once mobilised, Israel made winning back control of the Golan Heights the immediate priority. On the night of 8 October, Israeli tanks stormed the Syrian positions on the Golan. The Syrians had a surprise weapon, however: Soviet-made **infra-red** fighting equipment. This gave them the advantage at night.

ACTIVITY

Work with a partner to draw a concept map showing four reasons for early Arab successes during the Yom Kippur War.

SOURCE M

An Israeli soldier looks at an Egyptian Soviet-built SAM-3 missile launcher, captured during the Yom Kippur War. These missile launchers were crucial in protecting Egyptian forces from Israeli jets.

For 4 days, the fighting was fierce and losses mounted. However, Israeli tanks were superior and, by 10 October, the Syrian troops were in retreat. Israel's tanks pursued them into Syria itself, and were soon threatening the Syrian capital, Damascus.

Syria's president, Assad, appealed to Egypt to step up its attack in Sinai, hoping this would relieve the pressure on Syria. Sadat's original plan had been to occupy just a 15-mile strip of Sinai, aiming then to force Israel to negotiate and return Sinai to Egypt. Now, against the advice of his own generals, Sadat ordered his troops to advance. This was another lucky break for Israel because it meant that Egypt's forces moved beyond the protection of their SAM-3 missiles, making them vulnerable to Israeli air strikes. A massive tank battle took place in Sinai. 260 Egyptian tanks were destroyed; the Israelis only lost 20. It was a turning point. By the end of the second week of the war, the Egyptian forces had retreated to the Canal. Its 100,000 troops took up a defensive position there.

By 15 October, US military supplies had arrived in Israel. Strengthened, Israeli forces went on the offensive. Taking a bold risk, Israeli tanks led by General Ariel Sharon took control of a gap of around 1.5 km in the middle of the two Egyptian armies in Sinai. During a tough fight, he ordered 750 Israeli paratroopers to sneak across the Suez Canal. The next day, 50 tanks were floated over the Canal on inflatable rafts to reinforce them. Meanwhile, a massive mobile bridge was pulled across the desert by 12 Israeli tanks towards the Canal. On 19 October, the bridge was put in place and Israeli tanks and troops poured over the Canal. They quickly destroyed Egyptian SAM-3 missile sites, which meant that Israeli aircraft could now safely join in the fight.

Israeli tanks now controlled part of the west bank of the Suez Canal. By 23 October, one Egyptian army in Sinai was surrounded and had only 4 days of food, water and medical supplies left. They faced a desperate situation. Sadat agreed to a UN call for a ceasefire. Despite this, Israel pushed on into Egypt, looking to capture more land. The war now took an even more serious turn and it required international intervention to stop it (see Figure 3.9).

TENSION AND CONFLICT — THE MIDDLE EAST, 1917–2012

▶ **Figure 3.8** The Yom Kippur War

Map legend:
- – – – Bar Lev Line
- ➜ Egyptian and Syrian advances from 6 October
- ➜ Israeli counterattacks 11–24 October
- Israeli held land on the ceasefire 25 October
- Egyptian held land on the ceasefire 25 October
- Occupied territories

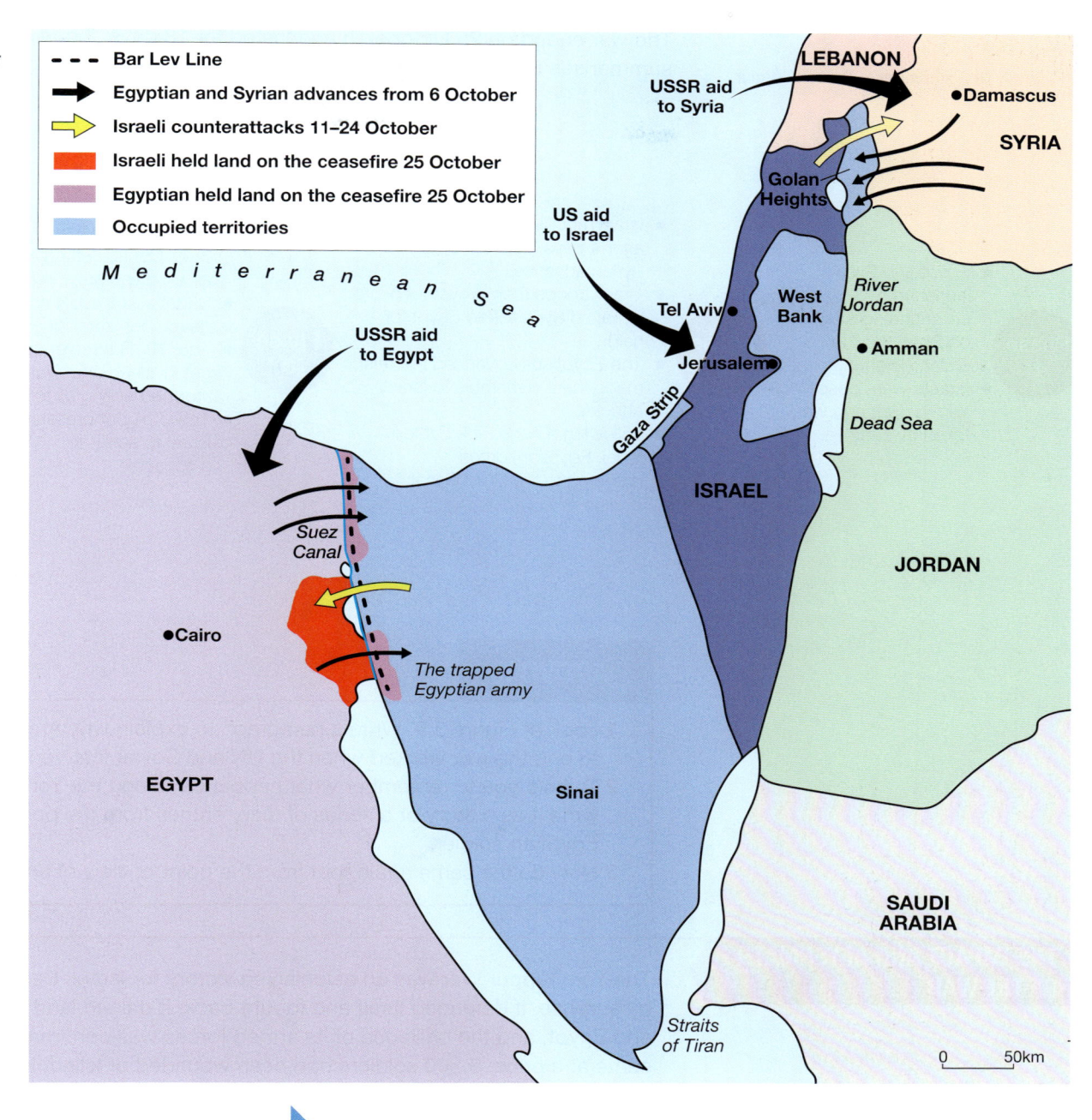

Map labels: Mediterranean Sea, USSR aid to Syria, LEBANON, Damascus, SYRIA, Golan Heights, US aid to Israel, Tel Aviv, West Bank, River Jordan, Jerusalem, Amman, Gaza Strip, USSR aid to Egypt, Dead Sea, Suez Canal, ISRAEL, JORDAN, Cairo, The trapped Egyptian army, EGYPT, Sinai, SAUDI ARABIA, Straits of Tiran. Scale 0–50km.

▶ **Figure 3.9** The end of the Yom Kippur War

UN intervention
- The UN called for a ceasefire.
- However, Israel pushed on to take more land in Egypt.

Soviet intervention
- The USSR told the USA that unless there was peace, they would send troops to help Egypt.
- The USA were determined not to let this happen. It went on nuclear alert.
- To stop the situation getting out of hand, the USSR backed down.

Arab intervention
- Other Arab states put pressure on the USA to stop Israel.
- They had a simple but effective weapon: they put an embargo on oil – refusing to sell it to the USA.
- The 'oil weapon' worked. Under US pressure, Israel agreed to the ceasefire.

Ceasefire

▼ Figure 3.10 A summary of the Yom Kippur War

The war ended on 25 October. It had lasted for 18 days. Figure 3.10 summarises the three main phases of the war.

Phase 1
- Egypt and Syria launched a co-ordinated attack on Sinai and the Golan Heights.
- Israelis were observing Yom Kippur and were taken by surprise.

Phase 2
- Israel mobilised and, after 4 days, halted the Syrian advance.
- Israeli troops then drove deep into Syria, so Syria asked Egypt for help.
- The Egyptians advanced but this made them vulnerable to Israeli attacks.
- Following a huge tank battle in Sinai, Egyptian forces retreated to the Suez Canal.

Phase 3
- Israel crossed the Suez Canal, cutting off an Egyptian army in Sinai.
- Sadat and the UN asked for peace but Israel ignored this.
- The USSR threatened to get involved and Arab states stopped selling oil to the USA.
- The USA put pressure on Israel to agree to a ceasefire.

Ceasefire

ACTIVITY

1 Look at Figure 3.9. Write a paragraph to explain why Arab intervention to end the war worked when the UN and Soviet interventions did not.
2 To help you to remember what happened during the Yom Kippur War, write it as a story or a series of diary entries from the point of view of an Egyptian soldier.
3 Now do the same again, but from the point of view of an Israeli soldier.

THE IMPACT AND AFTERMATH OF THE WAR

The Yom Kippur War was an astonishing victory for Israel. Despite being taken by surprise, it defended itself and fought back. It gained land in both Syria and Egypt, and the brilliance of its armed forces was confirmed. But victory came at a price: 9,500 soldiers had been wounded or killed. Israel had also suffered a blow to its confidence. Israel had survived and won, partly because of US support, and partly because of Egyptian and Syrian tactical errors. Most Israelis blamed their government for not being ready for an attack. The following year, Golda Meir and Moshe Dayan both resigned.

On the Egyptian side, the war seemed like a failure. Egypt suffered 30,000 casualties, its SAM-3 missile sites had been destroyed, and it had lost huge numbers of tanks and aeroplanes. The Suez Canal was still unusable. Hostile Israeli and Egyptian armies faced each other on its banks, while the Canal itself was full of debris from the war. However, Egypt gained a lot from the war. Overrunning the Bar Lev Line was a brilliant military achievement, and its Sagger and SAM missiles had done a lot of damage. Egypt could argue that it had only lost because Israel had US support. For the first time since 1967, Arab pride in its military ability was restored. More importantly, Sadat was now seen as a deserving successor to Nasser. He was in a stronger position to repeat his offer of 'peace for land'.

TENSION AND CONFLICT — **THE MIDDLE EAST, 1917–2012**

EXAM-STYLE QUESTION

AO1 **AO2**

SKILLS PROBLEM SOLVING, REASONING, DECISION MAKING

How significant was Soviet involvement in the changing relations between Israel and Egypt in the years 1956–73?

You may use the following in your answer:
- the Six Day War, 1967
- the Yom Kippur War, 1973.

You **must** also use information of your own. **(16 marks)**

HINT

The USSR's involvement took three main forms: aid, weapons and intelligence (like the false story in May 1967 that Israel intended to invade Syria). You could take these last two and show how they led to changing relations between Egypt and Israel. You then need to challenge the idea that the USSR was behind the conflict.

An unexpected impact of the war was to alert the USA to the need for peace in the Middle East. The quarrel between Israel and its neighbours could have led to the USA and the USSR going to war with each other. Also, the USA could not ignore the fact that it relied on Arab states for oil. What would happen if they refused to supply oil? (People called this 'the oil weapon'.) So, the USA had to rethink its support for Israel. Peace was more important and the USA had the power to force Israel to negotiate with Sadat.

The war had losers. Syria gained the glory of briefly overcoming Israeli defences and could be praised for the way it co-ordinated its plans with Egypt. But the Golan Heights remained in Israeli hands, and have remained so ever since. Palestinians gained no land back, even though many fought with the Syrians. Worse still, world attention was now focused on relations between Israel and Egypt, and who owned Sinai. Israel's occupation of the West Bank and Gaza, and the plight of ordinary Palestinian refugees, was ignored.

ACTIVITY

You have now studied four of the Arab–Israeli wars. To help you to remember them, create a copy of the following table, and fill it in. You will need to refer back to Chapter 2 to help you with the first two wars. When you have read Chapter 4, you can fill in the final column.

NO. DATE	1 1948–49	2 1956	3 1967	4 1973	5 1982
Name of war					
Who fought whom?	vs.	vs.	vs.	vs.	vs.
Who started it?					
Who won?					
What did the winners gain?					

RECAP

RECALL QUIZ

1. Name two decisions taken by Arab leaders at the Cairo Conference, 1964.
2. In which year did each of the following happen: the Samu Incident, the dogfight over the Golan Heights, the battle for Karameh?
3. Give two reasons for Israel's victory in 1967.
4. Name the five pieces of territory taken by Israel in the Six Day War.
5. Can you explain the following: Resolution 242, the War of Attrition, the occupied territories?
6. Which Palestinian group was responsible for: Dawson's Field; the massacre at Munich; raids from Karameh?
7. In 1973, who was in control of: Egypt, Jordan, Syria, Israel, the PLO?
8. What is Yom Kippur?
9. Give three reasons why the Israelis survived the Yom Kippur War.
10. Give two ways in which the Yom Kippur War changed global attitudes to the Arab–Israeli conflict.

CHECKPOINT

STRENGTHEN

S1 Summarise the events of the Six Day War.
S2 Draw a concept map to show the different examples of the tactics used by Fatah, the PFLP and the Black September Organisation. In a different colour, add Israel's reaction to each of these.
S3 Sadat's armies were defeated and surrounded in the Yom Kippur War. Give two reasons why he might nevertheless feel the war was a sort of victory.

CHALLENGE

C1 Which country do you think was most responsible for the outbreak of the Six Day War: Syria, Egypt, Jordan, Israel, the USA or the USSR? Explain your answer.
C2 Whose approach was more successful: Fatah's, the PFLP's or Black September's? Explain your answer. How successful were Israel's responses to Palestinian activities?
C3 How important was the involvement of the superpowers, the USA and the USSR, in causing the Yom Kippur War and then in stopping the war?

SUMMARY

- In 1964, Arab states set up the PLO and committed themselves to the destruction of Israel.
- With Syrian support, Fatah launched raids on Israel; Israel always retaliated to these raids.
- Syria and Jordan accused Nasser of not supporting Palestinians.
- Nasser's actions in May 1967 led many to believe that an Arab attack on Israel was about to happen.
- Israel decided to strike first and the Arabs were beaten in 6 days.
- After the Six Day War, the UN adopted Resolution 242, a 'land for peace' solution to the Arab–Israeli conflict.
- However, Israel annexed Jerusalem and imposed a military occupation on the other territories it had taken in 1967.
- Egypt began a War of Attrition against Israel, hoping to make it withdraw from the banks of the Suez Canal.
- Following 1967, Palestinians resolved not to rely on other Arab states. Different Palestinian groups used different tactics from raids on Israel to international terrorism.
- These tactics resulted in fierce retaliation from the Israelis, the expulsion of the PLO from Jordan and negative publicity. However, they also drew attention to the need to solve the Palestinian issue.
- On Nasser's death in 1970, Sadat took power, but he failed to persuade Israel to return Sinai.
- Sadat secretly planned a joint war with Syria against Israel.
- Israel survived the Yom Kippur War and gained more land.
- However, Sadat was now seen as a hero and he had broken the stalemate over Sinai.

EXAM GUIDANCE: PART (A) QUESTIONS

A01 **A02**

Question to be answered: Explain two ways in which the Yom Kippur War (1973) was similar to the Six Day War (1967). (6 marks)

1 **Analysis Question 1: What is the question type testing?**
In this question you have to demonstrate that you have knowledge and understanding of the key features and characteristics of the period studied. In this particular case it is knowledge and understanding of two wars.

You also have to explain and analyse historical events and periods to explain ways in which there were similarities between those events/periods.

2 **Analysis Question 2: What do I have to do to answer the question well?**
Obviously you have to write about the Yom Kippur War and the Six Day War, but you should not just write everything you know. You have to identify two similarities and provide detail showing how the wars were similar. If you just write narrative about the wars, you are unlikely to do this. So you should start by identifying two ways in which they were similar. (If you were encouraged to put subheadings in your answers, these two similarities would be your subheadings.) Then you need to provide detail to prove each of your points.

In this case, you might consider how the wars started and what the results were. You will get one mark for a similarity you show, one mark for explaining that similarity and another mark for detail.

3 **Analysis Question 3: Are there any techniques I can use to make it very clear that I am doing what is needed to be successful?**
This is a 6-mark question and you need to make sure you leave enough time to answer the other two questions fully (they are worth 24 marks in total). Therefore, you need to get straight into writing your answer. The question asks for two similarities, so it's a good idea to write two paragraphs and to begin each paragraph with phrases like 'One similarity was… ', 'Another similarity was… '. You will get a maximum of 3 marks for each similarity you explain, so make sure you do two.

Note: the question does not ask 'How similar', so you do not have to point out similarities and differences. Just stick to similarities.

Answer A
In 1967, Israel launched a surprise attack on Egypt, Jordan and Syria. In 1973, Israel did not expect Egypt and Syria to attack. A second similarity is that Israel won both wars.

What are the strengths and weaknesses of Answer A?
This answer has some merits. It identifies a similarity (Israel won both wars) and gives some support to the idea that both wars came as a surprise – but it doesn't support the similarity that Israel won, and doesn't set out the similarity on surprise. It is doubtful that this answer would score more than two marks.

Answer B
One similarity is that both wars started with a surprise attack. In other words, no ultimatums or warnings were issued. In June 1967, Israel launched a surprise attack on Egypt, Jordan and Syria. None of these countries were prepared for this. In October 1973, Egypt and Syria launched a surprise attack on Israel, which was taken completely unaware. Many troops were on leave and observing Yom Kippur with their families.

A second similarity is that Israel won both wars and made gains. In 1967, Israel captured East Jerusalem, which contained the Wailing Wall and Temple Mount (the two holiest sites for the Jews), the West Bank, the Gaza Strip, Sinai and the Golan Heights. In addition, huge amounts of Soviet weapons were captured, while the forces of Israel's enemies were completely destroyed. In 1973, Israel managed to drive back Egyptian and Syrian forces. In the north, it re-took the Golan Heights and extended its occupation into Syria. On the Egyptian frontier, Israeli troops pushed back the Egyptian advance, crossed the Suez Canal and occupied a part of Egypt.

What are the strengths and weaknesses of Answer B?
This is an excellent answer. Each paragraph begins by giving a similarity and goes on to provide factual support to explain that similarity. It would be likely to receive full marks.

Challenge a friend
Use the Student Book to set a part (a) question for a friend. Then look at the answer. Does it do the following things?

☐ Provide two similarities
☐ Provide detailed information to explain why they are similarities.

If it does, you can tell your friend that the answer is very good!

4. DIPLOMACY, PEACE THEN WIDER WAR, 1973–83

LEARNING OBJECTIVES

- Understand the oil crisis and the slow road to peace between Egypt and Israel
- Understand the significance of the invasion of Lebanon in 1982 for both Israelis and Palestinians

The 10 years covered in this chapter saw some appalling violence and misery: a worldwide economic collapse in the 1970s; the invasion of Lebanon (1982) and the destruction of its capital city; and massacres of refugees. There were more civilian casualties between 1973 and 1983 than in the previous four Arab–Israeli wars combined.

But this period also saw two very important peace initiatives. In 1974 Henry Kissinger, the US Secretary of State, persuaded Israel, Egypt and Syria to move towards better relations. Peace along the Suez Canal enabled it to be cleared, to the benefit of international trade. The uneasy truce between Egypt and Israel was then turned into a permanent peace in 1978–79 when, in return for Sinai, Egypt became the first Arab state to recognise Israel.

Connecting these two themes – violence and peace-making – were three things: oil, money and cameras. The need to undo OPEC's 'oil weapon', for example, fuelled Kissinger's 'shuttle diplomacy' in the 1970s, while financial aid – and the threat to withdraw it – played a role in pushing key players into making peace. And the role of cameras? The violence was reported around the world and seen for the first time on colour televisions. That made an impact: it focused attention on the plight of the Palestinian refugees and those living in the occupied territories; and it changed perceptions in Israel and America.

4.1 DIPLOMACY, 1974–75

LEARNING OBJECTIVES

- Understand the reasons why the USA tried to make peace between Israel, Syria and Egypt
- Understand the impact of Kissinger's 'shuttle diplomacy'
- Understand the significance of Arafat's 1974 speech to the UN.

THE SIGNIFICANCE OF THE OIL CRISIS

One reason why the 1973 Yom Kippur War (see page 63) ended was because **OPEC** used its 'oil weapon'. OPEC members refused to sell any oil at all to the USA, and they cut production for everyone else by 25 per cent. This quadrupled the price of oil, from $3 a barrel to $12 a barrel, which had an enormous impact because oil is used in the production of so many things. The fact that OPEC countries worked together in 1973 shows the strength of their feeling about Israel's advance into Egypt.

The restrictions on oil production (and the embargo on oil to the USA) continued after the end of the Yom Kippur War. By early 1974, the world was in the grip of major economic crisis, with **inflation** and high unemployment. This forced other countries, especially the USA, to rethink their approach to problems in the Middle East.

US INVOLVEMENT

The USA was very badly hit by the oil crisis. Although it had its own oil, it had to buy from the Middle East to meet its industries' needs. Unable to buy such oil, its economy was grinding to a halt. This meant the USA had a big incentive to make peace between Israel and its Arab neighbours, as then OPEC might relax its oil embargo. There was another good reason to make peace: the Yom Kippur War had almost dragged the superpowers into a confrontation. Another Middle East war could not be risked. Also, if the USA played the peacemaker, then perhaps Egypt and Syria could be encouraged away from the USSR's side in the Cold War.

KEY TERM

OPEC (The Organisation of Petroleum Exporting Countries) an organisation made up of major oil exporters, including the main oil-exporting Arab states such as Saudi Arabia. When the members of OPEC work together, they can make the price of oil very high (by cutting production) or very low (by producing a lot of oil). OPEC is powerful because its members control about 80 per cent of the world's oil reserves, and because the modern world needs oil so much

Gears diagram:
1. Huge rise in the price of oil
2. Production costs rise
3. Goods become more expensive
4. People buy fewer goods
5. Factories go bankrupt or lay off workers
6. High unemployment

◀ Figure 4.1 This diagram gives an example of the kind of economic impact that high oil prices can have on a country's economy. Keep in mind that high unemployment will mean people will buy fewer goods, causing more unemployment, and so on. It can create a vicious cycle

DIPLOMACY, PEACE, WAR — THE MIDDLE EAST, 1917–2012

ACTIVITY

1 Write a sentence defining the phrase 'oil weapon'.
2 Using Figure 4.1, explain to a partner why the 'oil weapon' had such a devastating impact on the countries targeted by it.
3 Put yourself in the position of an adviser of the US president during the oil crisis. Write a memo to the president to explain what action he should take to end the crisis and why.

KISSINGER'S 'SHUTTLE DIPLOMACY', 1974

KEY TERM

Secretary of State the US official in charge of foreign affairs

SOURCE A

US Secretary of State Henry Kissinger while he was engaged in his 'shuttle diplomacy'. Here he is flying between Alexandria, in Egypt, and Tel Aviv, in Israel.

The task of making peace between Israel and Egypt and Syria, fell to Henry Kissinger, the US **Secretary of State**. Since neither side would talk to the other directly, Kissinger played the role of the 'go-between' or intermediary. For 2 months, he flew back and forth between Israel, Syria and Egypt, a process that has become known as '**shuttle diplomacy**'.

Kissinger was in an excellent position to put pressure on Israel to pull its troops back since Israel was so dependent on US aid. He also found Egypt very willing to talk peace: Anwar Sadat needed to reopen the Suez Canal so Egypt could once more collect toll money (which had been worth about $220 million a year). Negotiations with Syria were trickier: President Assad did not want to lose face or back down on Syria's claim to the Golan Heights.

Kissinger did not achieve a permanent Middle East peace settlement. He was frustrated by the fact that neither Syria nor Egypt were prepared to recognise Israel's right to exist, and the new Israeli prime minister, Yitzhak Rabin, was not prepared to remove the IDF from either Sinai or Golan.

However, his shuttle diplomacy succeeded in a limited way. In January 1974, Egypt and Israel agreed to pull back from the Suez Canal and a UN peacekeeping force was installed between the two sides in a demilitarised zone (DMZ). Work could then start on reopening the Suez Canal. Both countries also agreed that they would settle any future conflicts by talking rather than fighting. In March 1974, in recognition of Kissinger's work, OPEC started selling oil to the USA again. Up in the Golan Heights, a DMZ was also created between Syria and Israel, patrolled by UN observers.

THE REOPENING OF THE SUEZ CANAL, 1975

Sadat's goal since 1970 had been to reopen the Suez Canal. However, the Suez Canal was in a terrible state. It was full of sunken ships and blocked by the causeway the Israelis had built in 1973. Its 164-km-long banks were covered with unexploded ammunition and minefields.

The banks were tackled first: 1,700 Egyptian troops worked for 3 months in the desert heat clearing 686,000 mines. During this dangerous work, 96 men died. It then took the united efforts of four navies (from Egypt, the USA, France and Britain) to clear the Canal itself. It was risky and challenging work. They lifted out 10,000 live shells, 10 major shipwrecks and a further 100 boats, 15 aircraft, 127 pontoon-bridge sections, and 600 obstacles like tanks and trucks, as well as the 12,000 four-ton blocks of concrete that made up the causeway. Finally, not even a grenade remained in the water.

72 DIPLOMACY, PEACE, WAR — THE MIDDLE EAST, 1917–2012

SOURCE B
The removal of the causeway over the Suez Canal built by the Israelis in 1973.

On 5 June 1975, exactly 8 years after its closure in the Six Day War, the Suez Canal was officially reopened. It was a very important event for Egypt and for world trade. Six hundred dignitaries attended the opening ceremony, which was held in Port Said. Amid the fanfare, Sadat – wearing a white admiral's uniform – boarded an Egyptian naval ship and sailed down the Canal.

ARAFAT'S SPEECH TO THE UN, 1974

ACTIVITY

You work for an online news agency and have been asked to write 25 words on what Arafat said, and 25 words on why his speech is important, for a post on the company news blog. What would you say?

The USA was not alone in using diplomacy to try to resolve the Middle East conflict. The UN also became involved, although for different reasons. In the early 1970s, the world had woken up to the fact that a dispute in the Middle East was making everyone vulnerable to Palestinian terrorism (see page 59). International pressure to understand this dispute and to find a solution grew. The trouble was that there was no single Palestinian leader with whom to negotiate. However, in October 1974, the Arab League recognised the PLO and its chairman, Yasser Arafat, as the only representative of the Palestinians. Then, in November 1974, the United Nations invited Arafat to explain Palestinian demands. The USA and Israel strongly objected to the invitation – Israel considered Arafat a terrorist and PLO raids on Israel were more damaging than ever.

SOURCE C
Yasser Arafat speaking to the United Nations in November 1974.

SOURCE D
Excerpt from Yasser Arafat's speech to the United Nations, November 1974.

Those who call us terrorists wish to prevent world public opinion from discovering the truth about us and from seeing the justice on our faces… The difference between the revolutionary and the terrorist lies in the reason for which each fights. For whoever stands by a just cause and fights for the freedom and liberation of his land from the invaders, the settlers and the colonialists cannot possibly be called terrorist, otherwise… the European resistance against the Nazis would be terrorism, … and many of you who are in this Assembly hall were considered terrorists… Today I come bearing an olive branch [a symbol of peace] in one hand, and the freedom fighter's gun in the other. Do not let the olive branch fall from my hand. I repeat, do not let the olive branch fall from my hand.

Nevertheless, Arafat gave a powerful speech stating the Palestinian view and received a standing ovation. In a significant move, the PLO was then given 'observer status' at the UN. Though it still could not vote, it could at least speak in UN discussions about the future of the Palestinians.

4.2 PEACE

LEARNING OBJECTIVES

- Understand the reasons why Sadat and Begin decided to make peace
- Understand the terms of the Camp David Accords and the Treaty of Washington.

SADAT AND BEGIN EXCHANGE VISITS, 1977

EXTEND YOUR KNOWLEDGE

JIMMY CARTER

Jimmy Carter was president of the USA from 1976–80. A very religious man, he believed that world peace was possible. He was the first US president to say openly that Palestinians should have their own homeland and worked hard to bring peace to the region.

Sadat needed to continue the peace process begun by Kissinger's 'shuttle diplomacy'. He wanted Sinai back and he wanted to solve the Palestinian issue. More importantly, however, he needed to achieve a permanent peace with Israel so that Egypt could recover from the costly wars it had fought. Its economy was in a bad way: in early 1977, food riots involving hundreds of thousands of people took place in Cairo. Sadat was also encouraged by an offer from US President Jimmy Carter: if Egypt made peace with Israel, the USA would help it with aid.

In November 1977, Sadat dramatically told the Egyptian National Assembly that he was prepared to go to the ends of the earth to find peace — even to the Knesset in Jerusalem. His challenge was accepted by the new Israeli prime minister, Menachem Begin. Begin needed an Israeli–Egyptian peace deal so that the IDF could focus on the PLO threat coming from Lebanon. Ten days later, Sadat visited Israel and spoke to the Knesset (parliament).

It was a huge step — he was the first Arab leader to even visit Israel let alone to propose a peace deal. It was also a risk, since most Arab leaders and all the Palestinians would see him as a **traitor**. However, Sadat believed that, if he could also negotiate a deal for the Palestinians, the risk would have been worth it. He invited Begin to visit Egypt, which he did in December.

In his speech to the Egyptian Assembly, Begin agreed to start peace talks with Egypt, but he made no mention of the Palestinians. Whatever Sadat might have hoped, Begin had no intention of returning the occupied territories or allowing Palestinian self-government. When the peace talks started in Egypt, disagreements over the Palestinian issue slowed them down. At that point, President Carter stepped in.

SOURCE E

Excerpt from Sadat's speech to the Knesset, November 1977.

I did not come to you with a view to concluding a separate agreement between Egypt and Israel… Moreover, no separate peace between Egypt and Israel could secure a lasting and just peace in the region as a whole. Even if a peace agreement was achieved, without a just solution to the Palestinian problem it would never ensure the establishment of the lasting, durable peace the entire world is now trying to achieve… We used to reject you, and we had our reasons… But I say to you today and I say to the whole world that we accept that we should live with you in lasting and just peace.

THE CAMP DAVID ACCORDS, 1978

President Carter invited Sadat and Begin to come to America and continue their talks at Camp David, the secluded country retreat of the US president. Since both needed US aid, they accepted.

SOURCE F

Menachem Begin, Jimmy Carter and Anwar Sadat at Camp David.

Camp David was a great choice: it was private, so the talks could be secret, and neither side could leave because access was by helicopter. To start with, Carter had to act as a go-between, moving from cabin to cabin. But he worked hard to create an informal, friendly atmosphere.

▶ Figure 4.2 The Camp David Accords, 1978

Framework for an Egyptian–Israeli Peace

- Egypt & Israel would be at peace.
- Israel would leave the Sinai within 3 years.
- Egypt would allow Israel to use the Suez Canal & Straits of Tiran.
- Egypt would receive $1 billion a year for 10 years from the USA.
- Israel would receive a $3 billion loan from the USA to help pay for the expenses of dismantling its bases in Sinai.

Framework for peace in the Middle East

- Israel accepted the legitimate rights of the Palestinians.
- Palestinians in the West Bank and Gaza could elect a council to govern themselves for 5 years.
- As soon as that had happened, Israeli troops would gradually withdraw from these areas.
- At the end of 5 years, a final decision about how these areas would be ruled would be made by Israel, Egypt, Jordan and the Palestinians themselves.

After 13 days, two agreements were reached, one concerning Egypt and Israel, and the other the Palestinians. The first agreement, the *Framework for an Egyptian Israeli Peace*, was very specific. However, the second, the *Framework for Peace in the Middle East*, was vague:

■ although Israel accepted the 'legitimate rights' of the Palestinians, it did not define what this actually meant

DIPLOMACY, PEACE, WAR — THE MIDDLE EAST, 1917–2012

ACTIVITY

1 Do you think Begin and Sadat deserved to win the Nobel Peace Prize? If only one of them could have won it, who would you choose and why?

2 In small groups, debate the following statement: 'The real hero of the Camp David Accords was Jimmy Carter.' Note down the best points raised in the debate.

- it did not mention Palestinians living in refugee camps outside the West Bank and Gaza
- it did not mention Jerusalem
- it did not mention Israel's occupation of the Golan Heights.

Worse still, the Palestinians had not even been consulted about the agreement.

When the Camp David Accords were made public, there were mixed reactions. Begin and Sadat were jointly awarded the 1978 Nobel Peace Prize. However, the UN rejected the *Framework for Peace in the Middle East* because it had not been consulted. Palestinians were furious, while other Arab states said that Sadat was a traitor and threw Egypt out of the Arab League. Many thought Carter was naive for believing that Begin ever meant to help the Palestinians.

THE TREATY OF WASHINGTON, MARCH 1979

Six months after Camp David, Sadat and Begin signed a **peace treaty** in Washington.
- Both agreed to recognise each state's right to live in peace.
- Israel agreed to withdraw from Sinai.
- Egypt agreed to allow Israeli ships to use the Suez Canal and the Straits of Tiran.

Both Begin and Sadat had what they wanted. Egypt had the peace and money it needed to rebuild, and Israel could focus on its border with Lebanon. As with Camp David, the treaty was met with international approval as peace in the Middle East seemed to be a step closer, but once again the Palestinian issue was not even mentioned. For that reason, Arab states and Palestinians strongly condemned the Washington Treaty, just as they had the Camp David Accords. As far as they were concerned Sadat had betrayed his own side.

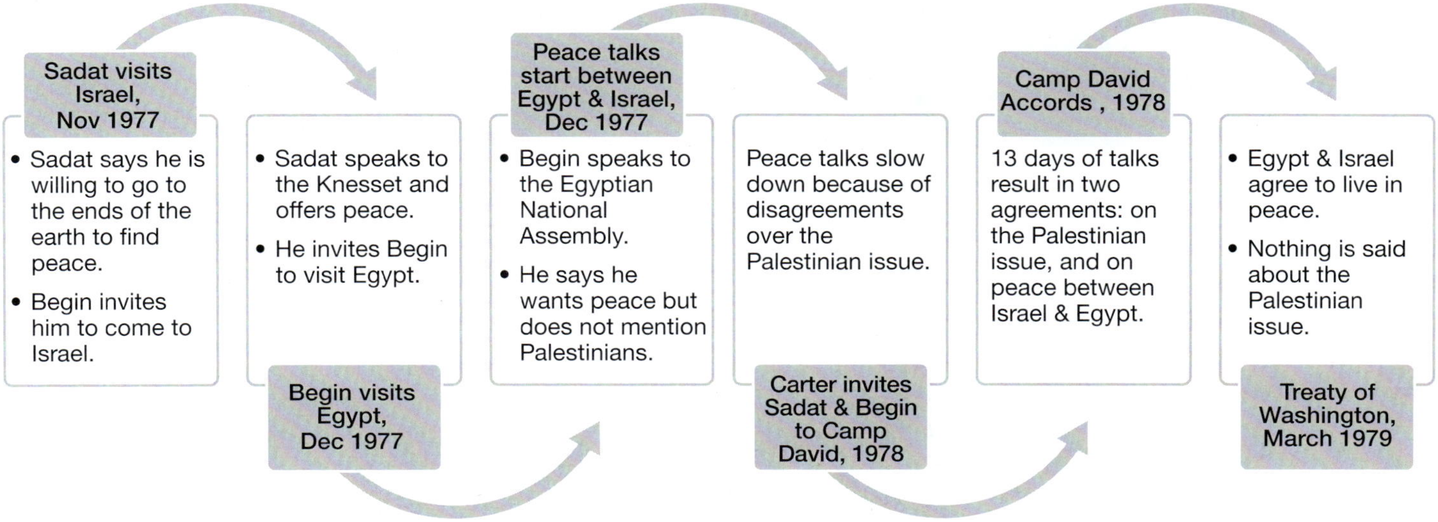

Sadat visits Israel, Nov 1977
- Sadat says he is willing to go to the ends of the earth to find peace.
- Begin invites him to come to Israel.

Sadat speaks to the Knesset and offers peace.
- He invites Begin to visit Egypt.

Begin visits Egypt, Dec 1977

Peace talks start between Egypt & Israel, Dec 1977
- Begin speaks to the Egyptian National Assembly.
- He says he wants peace but does not mention Palestinians.

Peace talks slow down because of disagreements over the Palestinian issue.

Carter invites Sadat & Begin to Camp David, 1978

Camp David Accords, 1978
13 days of talks result in two agreements: on the Palestinian issue, and on peace between Israel & Egypt.

Treaty of Washington, March 1979
- Egypt & Israel agree to live in peace.
- Nothing is said about the Palestinian issue.

▲ Figure 4.3 Egypt and Israel – the path to peace

DIPLOMACY, PEACE, WAR — THE MIDDLE EAST, 1917–2012

EXAM-STYLE QUESTION

A01 A02

SKILLS: PROBLEM SOLVING, REASONING, DECISION MAKING

How far did relations between Egypt and Israel change in the years 1956–79?

You may use the following in your answer:
- the Suez Crisis 1956
- the Camp David Accords.

You **must** also use information of your own.

(16 marks)

HINT
Make sure that you only cover the years given in the question. You don't have to use the factors given in the question (though it might be wise to do so). You must, however, bring in a factor of your own to show change or lack of it.

EXTEND YOUR KNOWLEDGE

PROBLEMS FOR CARTER
Jimmy Carter might have continued to work on the *Framework for Peace in the Middle East* and brought about a lasting solution, but two other foreign crises in 1979 then took priority – a revolution in Iran, during which 52 American diplomats were taken hostage, and the Soviet invasion of Afghanistan on Christmas Day 1979. The following year, he lost the presidential election to Ronald Reagan.

THE ASSASSINATION OF SADAT
In 1981, Sadat paid the ultimate price for making peace with Israel. During the annual victory parade held to celebrate Egypt's crossing of the Suez Canal at the start of the Yom Kippur War, he was assassinated by Egyptian Islamic militants who had infiltrated the armed forces. Despite this, Egypt's peace with Israel has continued to this day.

4.3 WAR

LEARNING OBJECTIVES

- Understand the significance of PLO activities in Lebanon
- Understand the reasons for Israel's invasion of Lebanon in 1982
- Understand the impact of this invasion.

One of the reasons why Begin was so keen to make peace with Egypt in 1979 was so that he could turn his attention to Israel's northern neighbour, Lebanon, where the PLO were based.

THE SIGNIFICANCE OF PLO ACTIVITIES IN LEBANON

When the PLO was expelled from Jordan by King Hussein following 'Black September' in 1970 (see page 58), it moved to Lebanon. For many of the 300,000 Palestinian refugees already in Lebanon, the arrival of the PLO was a real boost. Using money donated by other Arab states, the PLO set up schools and health clinics, repaired roads and provided electricity. It flew the Palestinian flag, taught Palestinian songs and poetry, and ran Palestinian youth groups. The PLO injected a new sense of hope and purpose into the refugee camps.

DIPLOMACY, PEACE, WAR — THE MIDDLE EAST, 1917–2012

SOURCE G

Fatah fighters on parade in Beirut, 1979.

EXTEND YOUR KNOWLEDGE

LEBANON

Lebanon's population is divided by religion and politics. In the early 1970s, about five per cent of the population were Druze, 40 per cent Christian and 55 per cent Muslim. Half of the Christian population were Maronites (a mainly Lebanese Christian group); the Muslim population was evenly divided between Sunnis and Shi'ites (the two main Muslim groups). Politically, Lebanese Sunnis looked for support from the other Arab states, while the Shi'ites looked to Iran. The Christians looked to Europe and the USA for support.

Keeping the peace between all these groups was difficult. When Lebanon became independent in the 1940s, a delicate power-sharing arrangement was introduced. The president was a Maronite, the prime minister a Sunni, the speaker of the parliament a Shi'ite, and the head of the army a Druze. With a lot of co-operation, the system of power sharing might have worked. However, the religious balance was upset by the arrival of Palestinian refugees, most of whom were Sunni. By 1970, one-tenth of Lebanon's population was Palestinian. Non-Sunnis, especially the Maronite Christians, felt increasingly under threat and resorted to violence to keep hold of their position.

However, for Lebanon's government, the arrival of the PLO was a nightmare. It saw the PLO as bullying, corrupt and arrogant. Yasser Arafat set up the PLO headquarters in the capital Beirut, and then established military recruitment and training bases in the refugee camps. The PLO acted as though it owned south Lebanon, which became known as 'Fatahland'. Even worse, PLO activities undermined the Lebanese government's efforts to stay out of the Arab–Israeli conflict. The PLO continued its cross-border attacks on Israel, and every raid drew a harsh Israeli reprisal.

Determined to destroy these PLO intruders, Lebanon's Christians set up their own paramilitary forces in the early 1970s, including the 10,000-strong, heavily armed **Phalange** militants. In response, Lebanese Muslims and **Druze** joined forces with the PLO. By 1975, the country had slid into a bloody civil war between all these groups. Over the next year, about 70,000 people died, while hundreds of thousands lost their homes and much of Beirut was destroyed.

The civil war sucked in Lebanon's neighbours: Israel supplied the Christians with weapons, while Syria went further and invaded. Syrian forces boosted the Christian militias and turned the tide against the PLO. By late 1976, though, the PLO still controlled much of the south of Lebanon, while the north was occupied by 40,000 Syrian troops.

KEY TERMS

Phalange the name of a Lebanese Christian right-wing political party in Lebanon, and also the name of its militia or military forces

Druze a small, close-knit, Arabic-speaking religious group that dates back to the 11th century. Their religious beliefs are kept a secret from the outside world

ACTIVITY

1. Why did the PLO move its headquarters to Lebanon in 1970?
2. What was the impact of the PLO's arrival? Write two lists, one showing any positive consequences, the other showing negative consequences.
3. 'The PLO's arrival brought disaster to Lebanon.' Write a speech arguing either for or against this statement.

RAIDS AND REPRISALS

> **SOURCE H**
>
> Excerpt from a speech by Prime Minister Menachem Begin, giving his reaction to the Coastal Road Massacre to the Knesset, 13 March 1978. He blames Yasser Arafat for the massacre.
>
> A day of bloodshed befell us last Saturday – a terrible day in the history of our people that will not be forgotten. The entire nation mourns its fallen – men, women and children – who were cut down by murderers merely because of being Jews. Merely because of being citizens of Israel…
>
> The murderers came from Lebanon. They were briefed by the head of the military wing of the Fatah organisation, the principal component of the organisation calling itself PLO – both commended by Yasser Arafat… Only three days ago that arch murderer was in Moscow where he was honourably received…
>
> Gone forever are the days when Jewish blood could be shed with [without punishment] Let it be known: Those who shed innocent blood shall not go unpunished. We shall defend our citizens, our women, our children.

In his speech to the UN in 1974, Yasser Arafat said he had an olive branch (a symbol of peace) in one hand. He was trying to suggest that the PLO was a reasonable organisation that would be willing to negotiate with the Israelis. Most Israelis refused to believe that he was genuine. Furthermore, many PLO members disagreed with Arafat's new approach. These 'Rejectionists' refused to accept anything less than the complete destruction of Israel. They had no intention of stopping their attacks on Israel.

THE COASTAL ROAD MASSACRE, MARCH 1978
On 11 March 1978, 13 PLO militants, all members of Fatah, decided to seize a luxury seaside hotel in Tel Aviv. The aim was to take the tourists as hostages to exchange for Palestinians held prisoner by Israel, and to wreck the Israeli–Egyptian peace talks then taking place. The militants arrived by boat 60 km north of Tel Aviv. They walked to a main road, hijacked a bus, and shot at passing cars as they drove to Tel Aviv. An Israeli police block finally stopped the bus. In the shootout that followed, 38 Israeli civilians, including 13 children, died, and a further 71 were wounded. It was the single deadliest terrorist attack on Israeli soil. Nine of the PLO militants were killed.

OPERATION LITANI, MARCH 1978
Israel's response to the Coastal Road Massacre was swift. On 15 March 1978, it launched Operation Litani and 26,000 troops invaded Lebanon. The aim was to take control of south Lebanon, to destroy PLO bases there and create a buffer zone that would protect northern Israel from PLO attacks. About 1,100 Palestinians and Lebanese died during Operation Litani, including 75 in a mosque that was destroyed by an airstrike. Most of those who died were innocent civilians because Yasser Arafat had ordered all PLO fighters to move north and out of the way.

GROWING TENSION, 1979–81
The UN quickly ordered a ceasefire and installed peacekeepers between the two sides. But these faced an almost impossible task, since they came under attack from Palestinian 'Rejectionists'. The Israelis preferred to put the task of patrolling the border in the hands of Lebanese Christians. But even they could not stop PLO attacks on Israel.

In fact, with Soviet help, the PLO grew stronger and stronger. It acquired heavy weapons from the USSR, including long-range artillery, rocket launchers and anti-aircraft missiles. Any IDF raid on a PLO base in Lebanon was answered with rocket attacks on Israeli farming settlements and towns in Galilee. By mid-1981, these attacks, reprisals and counter-reprisals were on such a scale that the PLO and Israel were effectively at war.

A UN-organised ceasefire in mid-1981 brought some calm but, as far as Israel was concerned, the PLO's possession of long-range weapons was an unacceptable threat. It used the truce to make plans for an invasion of Lebanon.

DIPLOMACY, PEACE, WAR — THE MIDDLE EAST, 1917–2012

ISRAEL'S INVASION OF LEBANON, 1982

On 2 June 1982, Israel got the excuse it needed to act when three Palestinians attempted to assassinate the Israeli Ambassador in London. The fact that the three assassins were not members of the PLO, and in fact were bitterly opposed to it, was ignored.

On 6 June, Israel launched Operation Peace for Galilee. With a massive force of 70,000 troops, 800 tanks and 350 fighter jets, it invaded Lebanon. Its aim, Israel claimed, was to stop further attacks by destroying PLO bases and establishing a buffer zone of 45 km in south Lebanon.

However, Israel soon went further than these aims. Israeli forces rapidly drove north, bombing towns as they went. 300,000 Lebanese lost their homes, 12,000 were killed and 40,000 wounded. Israeli forces then surrounded the Lebanese capital, Beirut, where the PLO had its headquarters. The aim was now (and probably always had been) to evict the PLO from Lebanon and to install the leader of the Christian Phalange Party, Bachir Gemayel, as president of Lebanon. He was pro-Israeli and would be a friendly neighbour.

Trapped, the PLO occupied residential areas in Beirut, hoping that the presence of civilians would deter the Israelis. It made no difference. For 2 months, Beirut was bombarded and food, water and electricity supplies were cut off. As the city was reduced to ruins, 20,000 innocent Lebanese civilians were killed.

SOURCE I
The bombing of Beirut by Israeli forces in 1982.

The removal of the PLO was the only way to stop the horror. In late August, a multinational force from the USA, France and Italy supervised the evacuation of 11,500 Palestinian fighters from Beirut by ship. Most, including Yasser Arafat, went to Tunisia. The PLO's headquarters were now in Tunis.

SABRA AND SHATILA MASSACRES, 1982

The Israeli Defence Minister, Ariel Sharon, was not satisfied. He announced that 2,000 PLO terrorists remained in the refugee camps. Two weeks after the PLO had been evacuated from Beirut, Israeli forces surrounded the two camps of Sabra and Shatila. They prevented anyone from leaving the camps, and then allowed in Christian Phalange forces to find any remaining PLO fighters. These Phalange forces were angry that 2 days earlier, their leader, the newly elected Lebanese president Bachir Gemayel, had been assassinated. A 2-day massacre followed, during which up to 3,500 civilians died, often after being brutally tortured. The Israeli forces surrounding the camps may not have committed these atrocities themselves, but they knew what was happening.

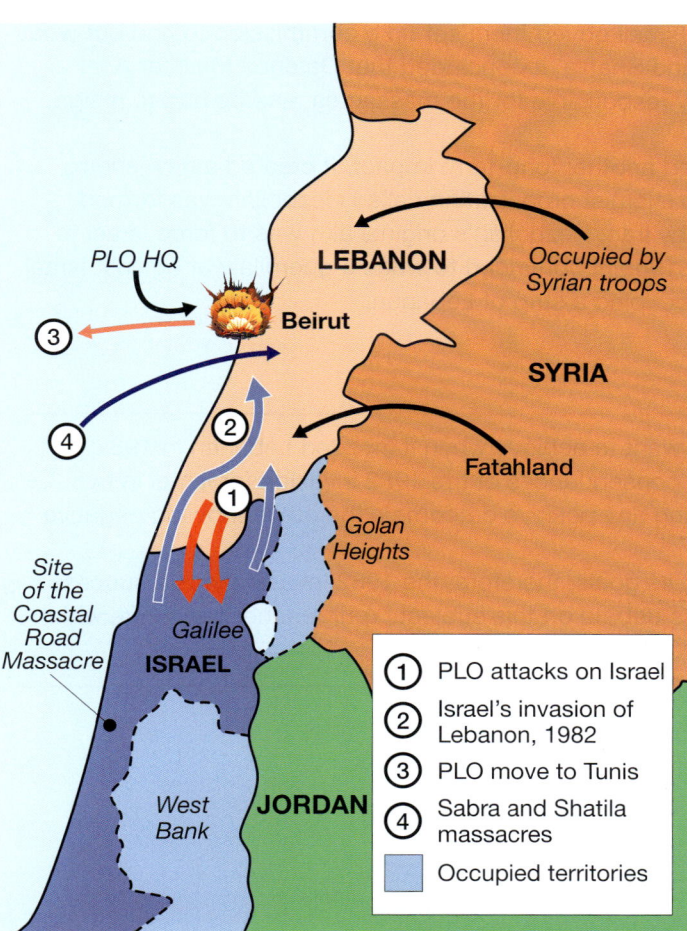

◀ Figure 4.4 Israel's invasion of Lebanon, 1982

EXAM-STYLE QUESTION

A01 **A02**

Explain **two** ways in which the Framework for an Egyptian–Israeli Peace was different from the Framework for peace in the Middle East. **(6 marks)**

> **HINT**
>
> You might, for example, consider the difference in the terms, in the amount of detail, or how much involvement the concerned countries had.

THE IMPACT OF ISRAEL'S INVASION OF LEBANON IN 1982

In one sense Israel achieved its objective: farms and towns in Galilee were now free from PLO raids and missiles. The PLO might not have been destroyed, but Yasser Arafat and the PLO leadership were now 2,400 km away in Tunis, which weakened their ability to damage Israel.

However, the war had negative consequences for Israel as well. It resulted in very damaging publicity, because Israel's methods had been so brutal. Towns and cities of Lebanon had been bombed, and many innocent civilians had been killed and wounded. Terrible weapons, like **white phosphorus** shells, had been used.

> **KEY TERM**
>
> **white phosphorus** a chemical substance that burns on contact with oxygen. Anyone exposed to white phosphorus smoke is seriously burned and their internal body parts are poisoned

The appalling massacres in Sabra and Shatila refugee camps resulted in international condemnation of Israel. These massacres also turned many moderate Israelis against the war. After mass protests involving more than 300,000 people, the Israeli government set up a commission to find out what happened at Sabra and Shatila. It concluded that Defence Minister Ariel Sharon was indirectly responsible for the massacres, and he had to resign.

The 1982 invasion had another long-term impact. It created a new enemy for Israel. In 1982, an Islamist organisation called Hezbollah was formed in Lebanon. Funded by Iran, Hezbollah's original aim was to force Israel to leave Lebanon. After 1985, it continued to wage a guerrilla war against Israel because Israel still occupied a strip of Lebanon.

> **ACTIVITY**
>
> 1 What did Israel want to achieve when it invaded Lebanon in 1982?
> 2 Summarise the consequences of the 1982 invasion for Israel in two lists, one showing any positive outcomes, the other showing negative outcomes.
> 3 'Israel achieved its goals; therefore, the 1982 invasion was a success.' Organise a class debate on this subject. Your teacher can judge which side has the stronger argument.

RECAP

RECALL QUIZ

1. Who was the US Secretary of State in 1974?
2. What was 'shuttle diplomacy'?
3. When did the Suez Canal reopen?
4. Give one reason why the UN invited Arafat to speak to it in 1974.
5. In what year did President Sadat visit Israel?
6. Where did President Jimmy Carter hold peace talks between Israel and Egypt?
7. Which Israeli prime minister made peace with Egypt in 1979?
8. What event led to the 1982 invasion of Lebanon by Israel?
9. Name the two refugee camps where massacres occurred in 1982.
10. Can you define the following: Druze, Phalange, Hezbollah?

CHECKPOINT

STRENGTHEN

S1 Create a timeline showing the development of diplomatic negotiations between Israel and Egypt in the period 1973–1979.

S2 Can you explain why Israel launched Operation Peace for Galilee?

S3 Draw a diagram that shows how and why international attitudes to the Palestinian issue changed in the years 1967–82.

CHALLENGE

C1 Explain why Sadat and Begin both felt the need to make peace. Why were other Arab states and the Palestinians so angry with Sadat?

C2 An event is significant if it results in important changes. Which event – the 1967 Six Day War, 'Black September' in 1970 or the 1982 invasion of Lebanon – was more significant for ordinary Palestinians? Which event was more significant for Israelis? Explain your answers.

C3 How important was the role of international media publicity in each of the events mentioned in C2 above?

SUMMARY

- OPEC's 'oil weapon' caused a worldwide economic crisis and prompted the USA to get involved in the Middle East peace process.
- Kissinger's 'shuttle diplomacy' resulted in UN-patrolled demilitarised zones between Israel and Egypt and between Israel and Syria.
- In 1974, Arafat was recognised as the sole leader of the Palestinians and spoke to the UN.
- In 1975, the Suez Canal was cleared and reopened.
- Sadat and Begin exchanged visits in 1977 and began peace talks. When their discussions slowed down, President Carter invited both to Camp David.
- The Camp David Accords had two parts: the first was about Egyptian–Israeli peace and led to the Washington Treaty of 1979; the second concerned Israel and the Palestinians, but was not implemented.
- Now based in Lebanon, PLO attacks on Israel continued, each resulting in a reprisal.
- Israel invaded Lebanon in 1982 to drive out the PLO, which moved to Tunis. However, Israel was condemned for its tactics.

EXAM GUIDANCE: PART (B) QUESTIONS

A01 **A02**

SKILLS ADAPTIVE LEARNING

Question to be answered: Explain two causes of Israel's invasion of Lebanon in 1982. (8 marks)

1 Analysis Question 1: What is the question type testing?
In this question you have to demonstrate that you have knowledge and understanding of the key features and characteristics of the period studied. In this particular case it is knowledge and understanding of the invasion of Lebanon by Israel, and why it happened.

You also have to explain and analyse historical events and periods to explain why something happened.

2 Analysis Question 2: What do I have to do to answer the question well?
Obviously you have to write about the invasion of Lebanon! But it isn't just a case of writing everything you know. You have to write about why it happened. To do this well, you need to give detail showing what caused the invasion to happen, but you need to make sure you are explaining why that detail actually led to the invasion. We call this explaining why your chosen causes produced the given outcome (i.e. the invasion of Lebanon in 1982).

In this case, there are many causes of the invasion of Lebanon. You might write about long-term or underlying causes like Palestinian attacks on north Israel from southern Lebanon, or you might write about the immediate event leading to the invasion, for example.

3 Analysis Question 3: Are there any techniques I can use to make it very clear that I am doing what is needed to be successful?
This is an 8-mark question and you need to make sure you leave enough time to answer the other two questions fully (they are worth 22 marks in total). Therefore, you need to get straight in to writing your answer. The question asks for two causes, so it's a good idea to write two paragraphs and to begin each paragraph with phrases like 'One cause was… ', 'Another cause was… '. You will get a maximum of 4 marks for each cause you explain, so make sure you do two causes.

How many marks you score for each cause will depend on how well you use accurate and factual information to explain why the invasion occurred.

Answer A

The underlying cause of the invasion of Lebanon was Israel's anger at the PLO. The PLO was making many cross-border and rocket attacks on northern Israel from Fatahland. Israel wanted to take control of south Lebanon, to destroy PLO bases there, and to create a buffer zone which would protect northern Israel from PLO attacks. The trigger came when three Palestinians attempted to assassinate the Israeli Ambassador in London – it gave Israel the excuse that it needed to go ahead.

What are the strengths and weaknesses of Answer A?
It has potential. It has the strength of setting out two reasons, and distinguishing between underlying and trigger reasons. But it hasn't provided much factual information to support those reasons, or fully explained why they caused the invasion. It is doubtful that this answer would score more than four marks.

Answer B

The immediate reason for the invasion of Lebanon was an event that happened in June 1982: three Palestinians attempted to assassinate the Israeli Ambassador in London. Israel used this as an excuse to launch the invasion – it was a reprisal attack on the PLO (although those involved were not in fact PLO members). So the attempted assassination had provided Israel with the justification it needed and the invasion began.

The underlying cause of the invasion was Israel's need to secure farms and towns in Galilee from the almost constant attacks they had suffered since the PLO had been ejected from Jordan and based itself in southern Lebanon. In March 1978, for example, a Palestinian raid resulted in the Coastal Road Massacre. These attacks then escalated in intensity and danger when the PLO secured Soviet aid, including long-range rocket launchers. By mid-1981, there were so many attacks and counter attacks that the PLO and Israel were effectively at war. The UN was meant to be in charge of keeping peace on the border, but it was powerless to stop them. So Israel invaded in order to destroy the rocket launchers, drive the PLO out of south Lebanon, and establish a buffer zone there that would enable people in Galilee to live in safety. This aim quickly grew into a decision to destroy the PLO in Lebanon completely, which explains why Israel carried its invasion right up to Beirut. The underlying causes meant that Israel felt the need to try to resolve the problems created by the PLO by carrying out an invasion of the Lebanon to expel it.

What are the strengths and weaknesses of Answer B?
This is an excellent answer. It gives two causes and provides factual support in showing how those causes brought about the invasion. It would be likely to receive full marks.

Challenge a friend
Use the Student Book to set a part (b) question for a friend. Then look at the answer. Does it do the following things?

- ☐ Provide two causes
- ☐ Provide detailed information to support the causes
- ☐ Show how the causes led to the given outcome.

If it does, you can tell your friend that the answer is very good!

5. THE ATTEMPTS TO FIND A LASTING PEACE, 1987–2012

LEARNING OBJECTIVES

- Understand why some Palestinians and Israelis came to accept the need to discuss peace
- Understand the attempts to bring peace in this period
- Understand why the resulting peace initiatives did not work.

During this period, there were some very important peace initiatives, but also an increasing number of civilian casualties. Worldwide sympathy for the Palestinian cause increased greatly because of the involvement of children in the First Intifada, an uprising in the occupied territories. Yasser Arafat announced that he no longer supported violence in 1988, and the PLO accepted Israel's right to exist.

Five years later, following the Iraq War and the end of the Cold War, Israel accepted the Palestinians' right to a territory of their own in the 1993 Oslo Accords. But the Accords did not bring peace and, in 2000, the Palestinians began the Second Intifada, which was a far more violent affair than the first.

The intervention of foreign powers in 2003 helped bring the Second Intifada to an end, but did little to solve key issues between Israelis and Palestinians. In particular, the conflict continued in Gaza, which in 2006 came under the control of Hamas, a Palestinian armed group whose aim was the destruction of Israel.

ATTEMPTS AT LASTING PEACE — THE MIDDLE EAST, 1917–2012

5.1 REVOLT

LEARNING OBJECTIVES

- Understand the causes of the First Intifada
- Understand the events of the First Intifada
- Understand the impact of the First Intifada on Palestinians and on Israelis.

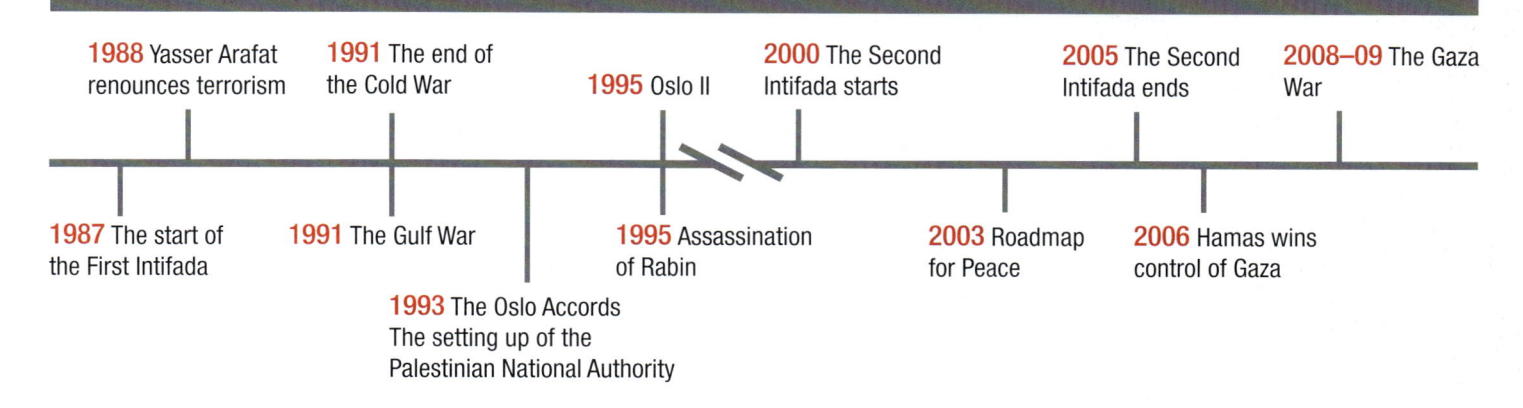

Timeline:

- 1987 The start of the First Intifada
- 1988 Yasser Arafat renounces terrorism
- 1991 The Gulf War
- 1991 The end of the Cold War
- 1993 The Oslo Accords. The setting up of the Palestinian National Authority
- 1995 Assassination of Rabin
- 1995 Oslo II
- 2000 The Second Intifada starts
- 2003 Roadmap for Peace
- 2005 The Second Intifada ends
- 2006 Hamas wins control of Gaza
- 2008–09 The Gaza War

LIFE IN THE OCCUPIED TERRITORIES

For ordinary Palestinians, life in the occupied territories of Gaza and the West Bank was harsh. Living conditions were crowded, basic and unhygienic. To make money, many Palestinians had to work in Israel, where they did unskilled jobs even if they were well educated. They had to pay Israeli taxes, but they had no say in Israeli government. They also had the daily humiliation of being under Israeli military occupation. PLO suspects experienced intimidation, beatings and random detentions without trial. Many endured sudden house searches and their land being confiscated. Some Palestinians feared that Israel planned to evict them completely, to make way for new **Jewish settlers** whose numbers were growing. There were 35,000 settlers in the occupied territories by 1984 and 64,000 by 1988. By the late 1980s, the Palestinians of the occupied territories could take no more. A single incident triggered a massive **uprising**.

KEY TERM

Jewish settlers Jews who lived in new settlements built in the West Bank and Gaza. For many very religious Jews, Israel's victory during the Six Day War was a sign from God that the Promised Land had been restored and it was their duty to settle in the West Bank and Gaza. Other settlers were encouraged to live in occupied territories by generous Israeli subsidies and tax breaks

SOURCE A

Children crossing overflowing raw sewage in the Jabalya Refugee Camp in Gaza.

THE FIRST PALESTINIAN INTIFADA, 1987–93

In December 1987 an Israeli market trader in Gaza was stabbed to death. The following day, an IDF truck crashed into two vans carrying Palestinians home from work, killing four of them and wounding seven. Rumours spread quickly that the crash had been a deliberate act of revenge. There was rioting at the funerals and an Israeli guard post was stoned. When another Palestinian was killed 3 days later, hundreds marched through the streets in protest. Within 2 weeks, the rioting had spread to the West Bank. A massive uprising, the *Intifada*, had started; it lasted for 5 years.

The Intifada soon **escalated** beyond rioting.

	▼ TACTICS	▼ ORGANISATION
At first	Mass demonstrations, barricades (barriers) on the streets, burning tyres and cars, anti-Israeli graffiti (wall paintings and slogans), throwing stones and petrol bombs at IDF troops, flying the Palestinian flag.	Leaderless and spontaneous.
Then…	In addition, refusing to buy or sell Israeli goods, refusing to work in Israel, refusing to pay taxes, refusing to carry identification, refusing to use taxis with Israeli number plates.	Organisation and co-ordination provided by a United National Leadership of the Uprising (UNLU). The UNLU distributed leaflets, telling people where to go and what to do, with messages about upcoming strikes and boycotts. It also co-ordinated underground schools, medical care and food supplies.

SOURCE B

Palestinians throw rocks at Israeli soldiers during violent protests against the Israeli occupation, 29 January 1988.

ATTEMPTS AT LASTING PEACE — THE MIDDLE EAST, 1917–2012

EXAM-STYLE QUESTION

A01 **A02**

SKILLS ADAPTIVE LEARNING

Explain **two** causes of the First Intifada (1987–93). **(8 marks)**

HINT

You could look at an underlying cause (for example, Palestinian anger about the quality of life they experienced in the occupied territories, or Palestinian concerns about the growing number of Jewish settlers) and at the trigger cause (the incident of December 1987).

The scale of the Intifada was extraordinary: in the first 6 months of 1988 alone, the IDF reported over 42,000 acts of hostility. That compared to an average of 3,000 a year before that.

Israel's response to the Intifada was severe. Prime Minister Shamir introduced an 'Iron Fist' policy.

- Reservists were called up and security was increased.
- Large numbers of schools were closed down, and curfews and **censorship** were put in place.
- Thousands were arrested, while suspected ringleaders were detained and their homes were bulldozed or blown up.
- The arms and fingers of child stone throwers were broken.
- Hostile crowds were dispersed with tear gas, rubber bullets and, sometimes, live ammunition.

SOURCE C

An Israeli soldier restrains another soldier from manhandling an arrested Palestinian, who has his hands tied together, 19 February 1988.

THE IMPACT OF THE FIRST INTIFADA ON PALESTINIANS

- 1,200 Palestinians were killed by Israelis, a quarter of them under the age of 16; 120,000 Palestinians were wounded (including 27,000 children).
- Another 882 Palestinians accused of working with the Israelis were killed by other Palestinians.
- Ordinary life became more difficult than ever as schools were closed for long periods, use of water was restricted, curfews put in place, and houses were knocked down without warning.
- The economies of the occupied territories were seriously damaged: businesses collapsed because of the curfews and strikes, and agriculture collapsed when olive groves were destroyed. Trade fell by 80 per cent and unemployment rose to 50 per cent.
- Many ordinary Palestinians felt a sense of empowerment; they were united in purpose and direction.

THE IMPACT OF THE FIRST INTIFADA ON ISRAELIS

- 160 Israelis died (100 were civilians).
- Israel's economy suffered: security costs increased greatly; closed borders and Palestinian boycotts damaged businesses; tourism collapsed.
- Israeli society became sharply divided: those on the right wing wanted to use even stronger measures to stop the disorder and to protect Jewish settlers, but many liberal and left-wing Israelis were shocked by the brutality of the IDF and some wanted to negotiate a peace.

SOURCE D

An Israeli settler in the West Bank describes what the settlers did if their cars were hit by stone-throwers.

A stone is thrown. Right there, the car stops and the passengers storm out and fire at the site from which the stones were thrown. They don't shoot in the air. They try to hit the person who threw the stones. There's no choice. You have to fire if you want to hit as many as possible.

SOURCE E

Adam Keller's reaction to the Intifada, as recorded in *The Palestinian Intifada Revisited* (2015) by Andrew Rigby. Adam Keller was an Israeli reservist who was arrested in 1988 for posting 'Stop the Occupation' stickers and spraying peace slogans on 117 Israeli military vehicles. He was demoted and given a prison sentence. On his release, he refused to serve in the IDF, giving this reason:

The IDF was founded as the Israeli Defence Forces, but it has become the Israeli occupation forces, an instrument to oppress another people. I refuse to be a smoothly working cog in that machine.

ACTIVITY

1. Look at Source C. How would you explain the actions of the soldiers in the picture? What do you think the Israeli soldiers are saying?
2. Shamir's 'Iron Fist' tactics were supported by some Israelis but opposed by others. What arguments do you think each side gave for their position?
3. Look at Sources D and E. How far do they prove that Israeli society became divided as a result of the Intifada? Explain your answer.

THE CONSEQUENCES OF THE FIRST INTIFADA

Media coverage of the Intifada resulted in a major change in international opinion. When images of children defiantly throwing stones at heavily armed Israelis flashed across the world, Israel's reputation suffered. Even Americans who had previously been on Israel's side were shocked by the tactics used by the IDF, while the UN condemned the 'Iron Fist' policy. There was now a lot of sympathy for the difficulties of ordinary Palestinians and a strong desire to seek a solution that helped them.

The Intifada was also a turning point for the PLO under Yasser Arafat. It led to a change of tactics (see below). Before the Intifada, the PLO's ambition had been the destruction of Israel; now Arafat proposed a two-state solution: the PLO would accept the existence of Israel, if Israel gave the Palestinians independence.

After 5 years, the Intifada finally forced the Israeli government to consider an alternative to its military occupation of the West Bank and Gaza. Attempts to crush the uprising were not succeeding and it could not afford to continue with the 'Iron Fist' policy for ever. It was expensive, damaging the economy and dividing society. The trouble was: what alternative was there? Annexing the territories – making them part of Israel – would not solve the problem, but handing them over to Palestinians would be strongly resisted by the settlers and those who believed that God had given the land to Jews.

5.2 ATTEMPTS TO ACHIEVE PEACE

LEARNING OBJECTIVES

- Understand why Arafat decided to recognise Israel and renounce terrorism
- Understand why the PLO and Israel finally agreed to negotiate peace terms
- Understand the role of the superpowers in the region.

ARAFAT RENOUNCES TERRORISM

KEY TERMS

Hamas Palestinian Islamic militant group. Hamas was set up 6 days after the Intifada started in 1987 and operated largely out of Gaza. Its aim was to destroy Israel and create an Islamic state and it used violent methods to achieve these aims, such as suicide bombings

Islamic Jihad Palestinian Islamic militant group. It was set up in 1981 with its base in the West Bank. Its aims and tactics were similar to those of Hamas

The Intifada took Yasser Arafat and the rest of the PLO leadership by surprise. They were based in Tunis, too far away to really control what was happening. For several reasons, Arafat decided a change in tactics was needed.

1. His leadership of the Palestinians was being overshadowed by new leaders in the UNLU (though they were largely loyal to the PLO) and new Palestinian terrorist groups, called **Hamas** and **Islamic Jihad**, which did not take orders from the PLO. Arafat needed to seize back the spotlight.
2. After 30 years of trying, he knew that the PLO ambition of destroying Israel was unachievable. Israel was simply too strong. Ordinary Palestinians needed peace, not a permanent struggle for an unachievable goal.
3. In July 1988, King Hussein renounced Jordan's claims to the West Bank. This meant that Arafat could propose the West Bank as the heart of a new Palestinian state.
4. The time was right for a new peace initiative. If Arafat could take advantage of the international sympathy for Palestinians, then something might be achieved.

In November 1988, Arafat announced a significant change in PLO policy. The PLO now recognised the existence of Israel and adopted a two-state solution – one state for an independent Israel and one state for an independent Palestine, which would have Jerusalem as its capital.

In December 1988, on the USA's insistence, Arafat made a speech to the United Nations renouncing and condemning all terrorism (see Source F). He was proving that he was genuinely interested in seeking a peaceful solution. He called for the withdrawal of Israel from all the occupied territories and asked Israel to join him in negotiations.

SOURCE F

Excerpt from the end of Arafat's speech to the UN General Assembly, December 1988. The UN met this time in Geneva since the US refused to issue Arafat with a visa.

I hereby address greetings to all Israeli factions, forces and sections led by the forces of democracy and peace… Come let us create peace – the peace of the brave – and move away from the arrogance of the strong and the weapons of destruction, and away from occupation, coercion, humiliation, killing and torture…

Finally, I tell our people: the dawn is coming and victory is coming. I see the homeland represented in your sacred stones. I see the flag of our independent Palestinian state flying over the hills of the dear homeland.

THE IMPACT OF ARAFAT'S SPEECH

Arafat's speech was important as it made the wider world aware of this major change in PLO policy. However, its immediate impact was mixed.

▼ POSITIVE OUTCOMES	▼ NEGATIVE OUTCOMES
The USA agreed to open negotiations with the PLO. The USA put pressure on Israel to negotiate with the PLO.	For Israel, the PLO were still terrorists and there would be no negotiations. Arafat's two-state proposal was also unacceptable. Arafat's peace initiative was also rejected by Hamas and Islamic Jihad. It was a betrayal of their objective: the complete destruction of Israel.

CHANGING SUPERPOWER POLICIES IN THE MIDDLE EAST

Despite Arafat's 1988 speech, and despite the Intifada, Israel refused to negotiate. It was a deadlock. But, over the next 3 years, this situation was changed dramatically because of events elsewhere in the world: the Gulf War and the end of the Cold War.

1: THE IMPACT OF GULF WAR, 1991

In the summer of 1990, Iraq invaded and occupied the tiny oil-rich state of Kuwait. The invasion was condemned by the world. In January 1991, a UN-approved, US-led coalition of 34 countries launched Operation Desert Storm and expelled the Iraqis from Kuwait.

This Gulf War, as it was called, might have happened over 1,200 km from Jerusalem, but it had a major effect on the Israeli–Palestinian deadlock. To start with, it was the first time that other Middle East states had openly

ATTEMPTS AT LASTING PEACE   THE MIDDLE EAST, 1917–2012

co-operated with the USA. As a result of the war, the USA was no longer viewed with such complete hostility, which put it in a stronger position to act as a peace negotiator between Palestinians and Israel.

Israel also emerged from the Gulf War with its reputation improved, at least in the West. During the Gulf War, Saddam Hussein fired missiles on Israel, hoping that Israel would retaliate and split the US-led coalition. An Israeli retaliation would have put other Arab states in a dilemma: should they be on the same side as Israel? However, even though the missiles destroyed over 4,000 Israeli homes, Israel did not retaliate. Its restraint was appreciated by the USA.

In contrast, the reputation of Yasser Arafat was severely damaged by the Gulf War. He made the serious error of supporting Saddam Hussein, who had always openly backed the PLO cause, and Palestinians cheered when missiles fell on Israeli targets. Saudi Arabia and Kuwait were furious. They withdrew their financial support from the PLO and, after the war, 200,000 Palestinians were expelled from Kuwait. By the summer of 1991, the PLO was discredited and bankrupt. Yasser Arafat's bargaining position with Israel, so high in 1988, was now weakened; he would have to lower his demands if he wanted to achieve anything.

▼ Figure 5.1 The Gulf War and the end of the Cold War

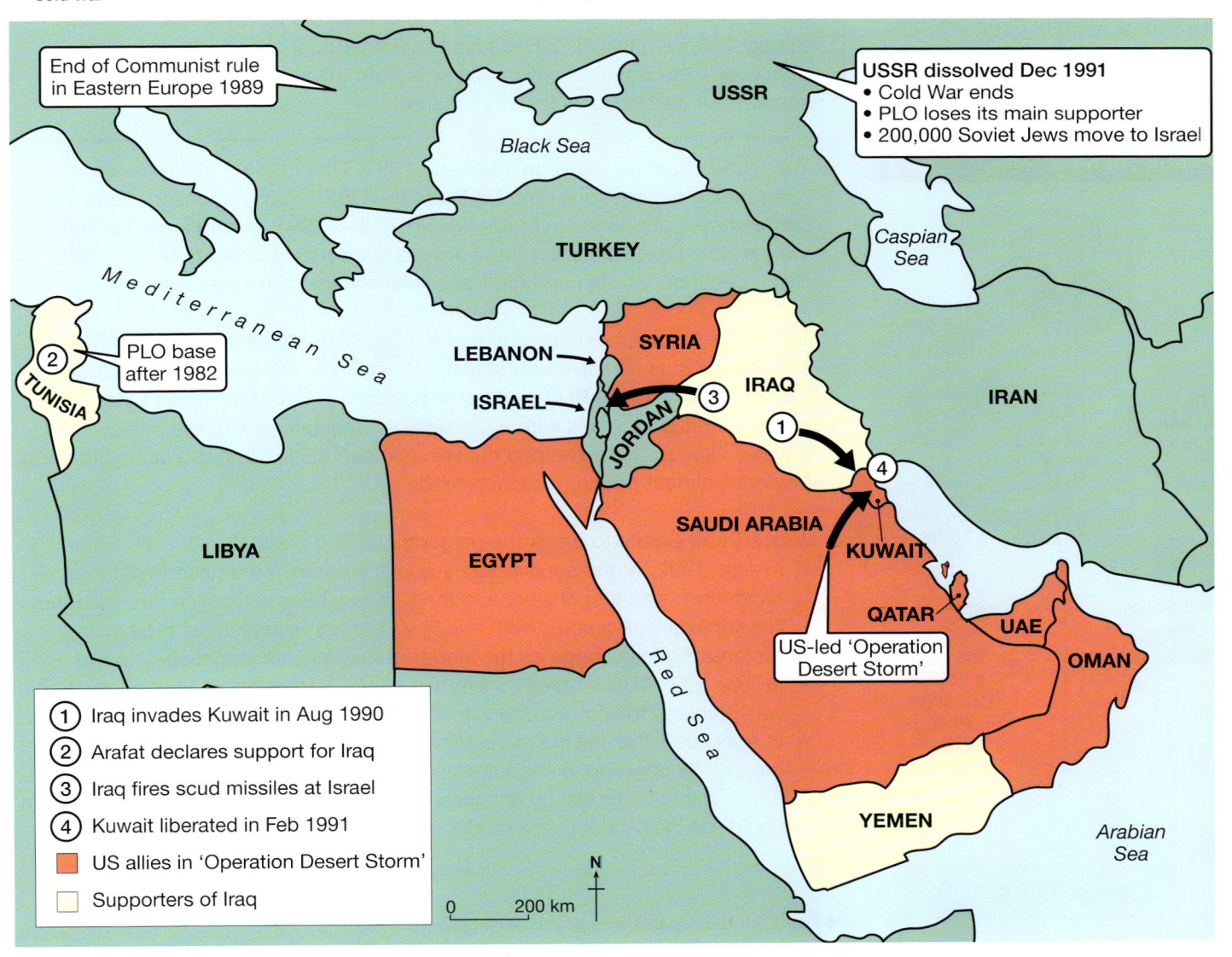

- End of Communist rule in Eastern Europe 1989
- USSR dissolved Dec 1991
  - Cold War ends
  - PLO loses its main supporter
  - 200,000 Soviet Jews move to Israel
- PLO base after 1982
- US-led 'Operation Desert Storm'

① Iraq invades Kuwait in Aug 1990
② Arafat declares support for Iraq
③ Iraq fires scud missiles at Israel
④ Kuwait liberated in Feb 1991
- US allies in 'Operation Desert Storm'
- Supporters of Iraq

2: THE IMPACT OF THE END OF THE COLD WAR

In late 1989, the USSR allowed communist control of Eastern Europe to end. Then, in December 1991, the USSR itself dissolved – the Cold War was over. These events also had a big impact on the Middle East.

The PLO lost its main source of finance and arms – the USSR – which further weakened Arafat's bargaining position. At the same time, he now needed to reach a peace agreement quickly because the collapse of the USSR also resulted in 200,000 Soviet Jews migrating to Israel. Israel started to build settlements for this new wave of immigrants in the West Bank. Arafat knew that the more settlements there were, the more difficult it would be to recover the whole of the West Bank for Palestinians. The arrival of the Soviet Jews also had a negative impact on the economies of the West Bank and Gaza. Before 1989, one-third of Palestinians earned their living by working in Israel; now they were not needed. For all these reasons, Arafat needed to reach an agreement as soon as possible, even if it meant settling for less than he wanted.

Israel was also affected negatively by the collapse of the USSR. During the Cold War, it had been the USA's only ally in the Middle East. But the USA was now the only superpower: it did not need Israel in the same way. By threatening to withhold financial aid, the USA could put pressure on Israel to negotiate with the PLO. Because Israel needed that financial aid more than ever – the wave of new immigrants from the USSR needed housing and schools – it had to do as the USA wished.

ACTIVITY

In 1988, Arafat's negotiating position was strong; by 1993, it was weak. Working with a partner, identify three reasons for this change. Which of these was the most important?

PEACE TALKS

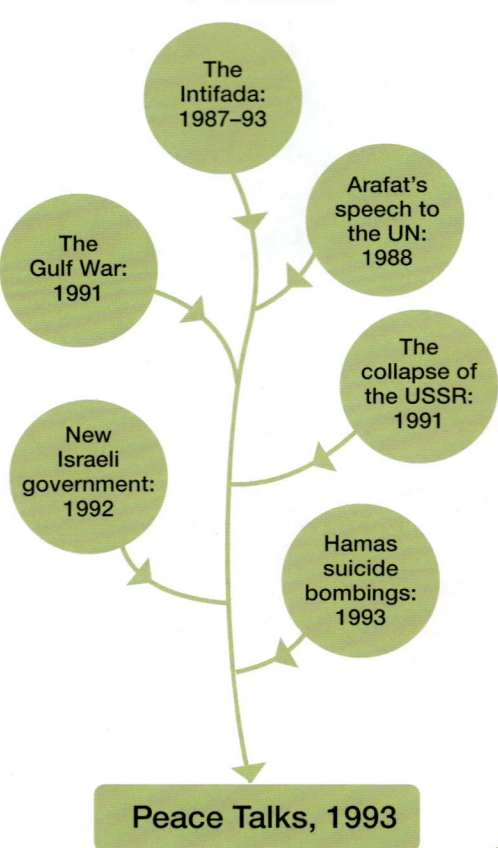

The world changed between 1988 and 1991. That made it much easier to open peace negotiations. The USA and the USSR jointly sponsored a peace conference that opened in Madrid in November 1991. Because of the Gulf War, Middle East states like Saudi Arabia supported the conference. Israel, Syria, Lebanon, Jordan and the Palestinians were all invited to attend.

The peace talks almost failed at the first hurdle. Israel refused to talk with any Palestinians who lived outside the West Bank and Gaza. That excluded Yasser Arafat and the PLO leadership based in Tunis. Meanwhile, Lebanon and Syria refused to talk with Israel unless Israel talked with the Palestinians. It was a vicious circle. Despite numerous meetings in Madrid, Washington and Moscow, almost nothing was achieved.

It took three events to break the deadlock.

- In April 1992, Arafat survived an aeroplane crash in the deserts of Libya. A sandstorm was responsible and for 12 hours people thought he was dead. His survival was greeted with relief by ordinary Palestinians: the crash restored Arafat's image as the leader of the Palestinian cause.
- In June 1992, a new Israeli government led by Yitzhak Rabin took power. Rabin was prepared to compromise with the PLO if it meant ending the Intifada.
- In April 1993, the first Hamas suicide bombing took place in Israel. Hamas was completely unwilling to negotiate with Israel. It saw the Palestinian struggle as a holy war to be fought by any means possible. Compared with Hamas, Rabin could see that Arafat was a moderate who could be negotiated with.

Figure 5.2 The impact of changes between 1987–93

ATTEMPTS AT LASTING PEACE — THE MIDDLE EAST, 1917–2012

ACTIVITY

In 1988, Israel refused to negotiate with Palestinians; in 1993, it agreed to negotiate. Working with a partner, identify three reasons for this change in policy. Which of these was the most important?

However, although Rabin and Arafat were prepared to talk, neither could risk doing so openly. On each side there were those who would see any compromise as betrayal:
- if Rabin gave away any of the West Bank, the settlers would be furious
- if Arafat accepted less than the whole of the West Bank, hard-line Palestinians would be furious.

5.3 ARAFAT, RABIN AND THE OSLO PEACE ACCORDS

LEARNING OBJECTIVES

- Understand the terms of the Oslo Peace Accords (1993) and Oslo II (1995)
- Understand Netanyahu's opposition to the Accords
- Understand why the Accords did not result in a lasting peace.

EXTEND YOUR KNOWLEDGE

THE WORK OF THE PNA

To start with, the PNA ruled over Gaza (except Jewish settlements), and the town of Jericho in the West Bank. In 1995, Israel handed over a further five towns in the West Bank to PNA control. The first elections were held in 1996. Following a Fatah victory, Yasser Arafat became the first president of the PNA. One of the PNA's first moves was to double the number of teachers to 20,000 and create a police force of 30,000. Because of these moves, it became the largest employer in Gaza and the West Bank. Its power also rested on the fact that it controlled all foreign aid to Palestinians.

KEY TERM

Palestinian National Authority a kind of governmental body responsible for internal affairs in Palestine such as education, culture, health, social welfare, taxation and tourism. It was also responsible for creating a Palestinian police force to maintain law and order, and prevent acts of terrorism against Israel from Gaza or the West Bank

Top secret talks began in Oslo, the capital of Norway. Even the USA was not aware that they were happening. Rabin and Arafat sent moderate representatives to Oslo. In other words, both sides were really trying to reach an agreement. But the real star of these talks was their host, the Norwegian Foreign Minister Johan Jorgen Holst. Holst felt that a relaxed friendly atmosphere would help make the negotiations work. So he held the talks in remote farmhouses and in his own home in Oslo, where his four-year-old son broke the ice by playing with the Israeli and Palestinian negotiators.

After days of difficult negotiations, both sides agreed to the Oslo Accords. These were not a final peace treaty, but a joint commitment to work at finding a solution over the next 5 years.
- Israel accepted the PLO as the representative of the Palestinian people, and Arafat could return from Tunis.
- The PLO renounced violence and accepted Israel's right to exist.
- Both sides agreed that a **Palestinian National Authority** (PNA) should be set up; this would be run by the PLO at first but, eventually, its members would be democratically elected by Palestinians living in the West Bank and Gaza.
- Over the next 5 years, Israeli forces would gradually withdraw from parts of the West Bank, and transfer responsibility for governing these parts to the PNA.
- At the same time, negotiations would take place on difficult issues like where the borders should be, what to do about Israeli settlers and Palestinian refugees in neighbouring countries, and who controlled Jerusalem.
- A permanent peace treaty would then be signed at the end of the five-year period.

ATTEMPTS AT LASTING PEACE — THE MIDDLE EAST, 1917–2012

EXTEND YOUR KNOWLEDGE

JOHAN JORGEN HOLST
The hero behind the Oslo Accords did not live to see the 1994 Nobel Peace Prize ceremony. Exhausted from the role he had played in the Oslo negotiations, the Norwegian foreign minister suffered a stroke in December 1993. He died a month later.

The Oslo Accords were a breakthrough. There was a real sense of optimism that this time there could be peace. Each side would gain. Palestinians would get land and an opportunity to rebuild their economy, while Israel would get peace and security from terrorist attacks. In September 1993, Rabin and Arafat met in Washington to sign the Accords. The following year, they were jointly awarded the Nobel Peace Prize for their efforts to create peace in the Middle East.

SOURCE G

Yitzhak Rabin, Bill Clinton and Yasser Arafat meet at the White House to sign the Oslo Accords, 1993. This was the first time that Rabin and Arafat had ever shaken hands.

OSLO II, 1995

The Oslo Accords of 1993 were rather vague about which 'parts' of the West Bank and Gaza would come under PNA control, but that was made clear 2 years later. While Gaza would eventually be completely Palestinian, the Oslo II Accords divided the West Bank into three parts.

- Area A was controlled totally by the PNA. It contained eight Palestinian cities and their surrounding areas, amounting to about 3 per cent of the West Bank. No Israelis were allowed to enter Area A. The PNA would prevent terrorist attacks on Israel from this area.
- Area B was under joint Palestinian civil control and Israeli military control. It contained about 440 Palestinian villages and their surrounding lands, amounting to about 25 per cent of the West Bank. There were no Israeli settlements in Area B. Israeli forces would be gradually withdrawn once security issues had been resolved.
- Area C was the rest of the West Bank. It was controlled totally by Israel. There were about 110,000 Jewish settlers in this area. Parts of this area would be gradually transferred to Palestinian control.

ATTEMPTS AT LASTING PEACE — THE MIDDLE EAST, 1917–2012

▶ **Figure 5.3** Oslo II and the division of the West Bank

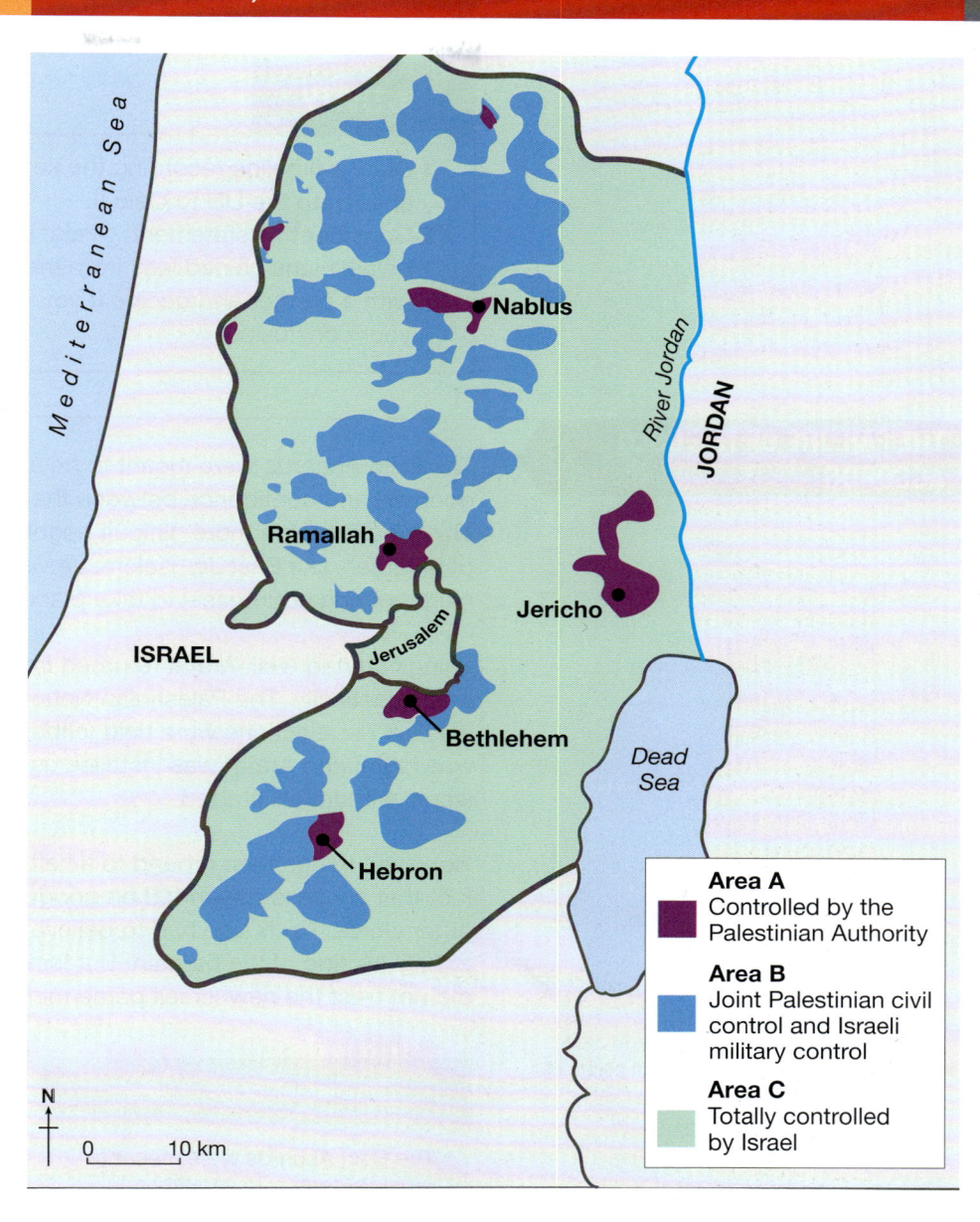

[Map showing the West Bank divided into three areas:
- *Area A — Controlled by the Palestinian Authority*
- *Area B — Joint Palestinian civil control and Israeli military control*
- *Area C — Totally controlled by Israel*

Labelled locations: Nablus, Ramallah, Jerusalem, Jericho, Bethlehem, Hebron. Surrounding features: Mediterranean Sea, River Jordan, Dead Sea, Israel, Jordan.]

REACTIONS TO THE OSLO PEACE ACCORDS

Oslo II shocked many on both sides. Moderate Palestinians who had been optimistic in 1993 now objected to the fact that so much of the West Bank was still going to be in Israeli hands. Furthermore, Area C contained most of the West Bank's natural resources, and movement between Areas A and B would be difficult. (The PFLP, Hamas and Islamic Jihad had always refused to accept anything less than the total destruction of Israel.)

On the other side, many Israelis were delighted by the prospect of peace. However, Israeli settlers strongly objected to giving up any part of 'Biblical Israel' at all. They saw Rabin as a traitor. Two months after Oslo II was signed, he was assassinated by an Israeli-Jewish religious extremist called Yigal Amir. Rabin's death stunned the Israeli public and hundreds of thousands gathered to light candles in his memory. Rabin's funeral was attended by many world leaders, including President Clinton of the USA, King Hussein of Jordan and President Mubarak of Egypt.

ACTIVITY

1. Draw a timeline recording the key events of 1988 to 1995, from Arafat's speech to the UN to Oslo II.
2. Consider this statement: 'Arafat's weak bargaining position meant the Palestinians gained less from the Oslo Accords than the Israelis.' Work with a partner and decide if you agree. Write a paragraph to explain your conclusion.

THE FAILURE OF THE OSLO ACCORDS

The Oslo Accords were meant to be an interim agreement that would build goodwill and confidence between the two sides over a five-year period. This would enable more difficult negotiations on the major remaining issues of dispute – like East Jerusalem, Jewish settlers, borders and refugees in neighbouring countries – to take place and result in a final agreement.

Things started well. Arafat returned from Tunis and was greeted enthusiastically. The Palestinian National Authority was set up; the police force was set up; elections were held (although boycotted by Hamas, voting turnout was high); and Arafat was installed as president in 1996. The slow process of Israeli withdrawal started.

However, things then ground to a halt. The key reason for this failure lay in the fact that success depended on goodwill between the leaders of each side. In other words, each side had to believe that the other side was genuinely trying to fulfil its side of the bargain. But Israelis did not trust Arafat, and Palestinians did not trust the new Israeli prime minister.

▶ Figure 5.4 Israeli and Palestinian points of view

The Israeli point of view	The Palestinian point of view
• The Oslo Accords were meant to provide Israel with security and peace. • However, Arafat could not or would not stop terrorist attacks on Israel. He did not disarm the PFLP, Hamas or Islamic Jihad terrorists, so Israel felt that Arafat had not fulfilled his side of the bargain. • It therefore took measures to stop the movement of terrorists and their weapons: it established road blocks between Palestinian cities and prevented contact between Gaza and the West Bank. • It also continued building and expanding Jewish settlements in Area C of the West Bank. • The lack of economic development in the West Bank and Gaza was Arafat's fault: he was corrupt so donors stayed away, and he rejected UN reconstruction plans.	• The Oslo Accords were meant to provide Palestinians with land and a chance to rebuild their economy. • However, Oslo II only gave them full control of 3% of the West Bank. • Movement between Palestinian towns and villages remained very difficult because of Israeli roadblocks. This hampered economic development. • Because Israel permitted more Jewish settlements in Area C, it was unlikely that Palestinians would ever get full control over the rest. • Economic reconstruction in Gaza and the West Bank also stalled because the UN reconstruction plans meant losing authority to outsiders, which Arafat was reluctant to accept.

ATTEMPTS AT LASTING PEACE — THE MIDDLE EAST, 1917–2012

NETANYAHU'S OPPOSITION TO OSLO

SOURCE H

Excerpt from an article by Professor Avi Shlaim of Oxford University, written in 2013.

[Netanyahu] made no effort to conceal his deep antagonism to Oslo, denouncing it as incompatible with Israel's right to security and with the historic right of the Jewish people to the whole land of Israel. And he spent his first three years as [prime minister] in a largely successful attempt to arrest, undermine, and subvert the accords.

When Rabin was killed, his deputy, Shimon Peres, called an election and most expected him to win. But, just before the election, Hamas carried out a suicide bombing, killing 32 Israelis. Peres, the peacemaker, seemed weak and lost support. Israelis voted in the right-wing candidate, Benjamin Netanyahu, who was anti-Oslo and pro-settler. In power, Netanyahu took a subtle approach. He could not reject Oslo outright without losing US support. Instead, he demanded hard evidence of Palestinian goodwill before Israel made any concessions. Meanwhile, he allowed further Jewish settlements. This approach paralysed the peace process.

In a downward spiral of claims and counterclaims that each side was violating the Oslo Accords, the optimism and goodwill that had existed in 1993 had vanished by 2000. US President Clinton tried to rescue the situation by inviting both sides to Camp David for peace talks, but these collapsed. Oslo was dead.

EXTEND YOUR KNOWLEDGE

BENJAMIN NETANYAHU

Nicknamed 'Bibi', Netanyahu was born in 1949, making him the first Israeli prime minister to be born in Israel. He studied in the USA, and served in the IDF during the Six Day War, the War of Attrition and the Yom Kippur War. His brother died in 1976 leading Operation Entebbe, a mission to rescue Jews who were held hostage on a hijacked aeroplane. Netanyahu entered politics in 1988, and became leader of Likud, the right-wing party founded by Menachem Begin, in 1993. He won the 1996 election – but lost support and 'retired' in 1999, when he became caught up in a wave of personal scandals and corruption charges. He returned to politics in 2009, and won the 2009, 2013 and 2015 elections.

EXAM-STYLE QUESTION

AO1 AO2

SKILLS ▶ ADAPTIVE LEARNING

Explain **two** causes of the failure of the Oslo Peace Accords of 1993–95.

(8 marks)

HINT

This question is testing your ability to explain why an event happened. A good answer would start with the words 'The Oslo Peace Accords failed because… ', then give a reason, and then provide some evidence. Remember to write about two causes.

5.4 THE SECOND INTIFADA, 2000–05

LEARNING OBJECTIVES

- Understand how and why the Second Intifada was different from the First Intifada
- Understand how Israel reacted to the Second Intifada.

In this tense atmosphere, a single 45-minute incident triggered a Second Intifada. Ariel Sharon, the new head of the Israeli opposition party Likud, visited Temple Mount in Jerusalem. Surrounded by riot police, he was making a provocative statement: the heart of Jerusalem was Jewish and would be Israeli. But, from the Palestinian point of view, he was acting illegally, and insulting Islam's third holiest site. Sharon was already hated by Palestinians for the 1982 massacres that happened during Israel's invasion of Lebanon.

Thousands of Palestinians protested. They threw missiles; the Israeli police retaliated with tear gas and rubber bullets. Fighting quickly turned into widespread violence.

SOURCE I

Crowds demonstrating at the start of the Second Intifada. Here West Bank Palestinians carry Hezbollah flags and an image of 12-year-old Muhammad al-Doura and his father. The pair were trying to shelter from gunfire in Gaza in September 2000 when Muhammad was killed.

The Second Intifada was far more violent and brutal than the First. Ten years earlier, Palestinians had hurled rocks and insults. Now they used knives, bullets, grenades, rockets, mortars and suicide bombings. The suicide bombers struck the most fear into Israelis. Targeting buses, discos, restaurants, crowded shopping streets – anywhere there was a crowd – they caused chaos and severe casualties.

Several factors may explain this new level of violence on the Palestinian side.

▼ Figure 5.5 Factors sparking greater violence

Anger and frustration	Inspiration	Arafat's weakness	Provocation	Jihadism	Outside support	Rivalry
• Palestinians were frustrated about the lack of progress since Oslo. • They were angered by Israel's support for new settlers, and by corruption on their own side.	• Many Palestinians believed that Hezbollah's guerrilla campaign had forced Israel to pull out of Lebanon in May 2000. • They hoped to achieve the same result.	• He did not control Islamic Jihad or Hamas, and a new younger generation was ambitious to take his place. • He secretly supported the Al-Aqsa Martyrs' Brigades, which had many Fatah members, because he needed to show he was in charge.	• Israel suppressed the riots of September 2000 violently: before an Israeli had been killed, the IDF had fired 1.3 million bullets. • Over the next 4 years incidents like the death of Muhammad al-Doura caused very strong feelings.	• Following 9/11 a new wave of radical Islamism swept the world. • Many Palestinians were inspired by Osama bin Laden to see Israel as evil and that it had to be destroyed. • Those who died were hailed as martyrs.	• The weapons used – grenades, rockets, mortars – came from abroad. • Iran funded Islamic Jihad.	• Confusingly, there were many different Palestinian armed groups including the PFLP, Islamic Jihad, Hamas, and Al-Aqsa Martyrs' Brigades. • There was almost a competition between these to be the deadliest, and therefore the most influential.

ARIEL SHARON'S RESPONSE TO THE SECOND INTIFADA

EXTEND YOUR KNOWLEDGE

'BLACK MARCH' 2002
The impact of suicide bombings on Israeli civilians in 1 month:

- 2 March: 11 killed and 50 injured at a family celebration in Jerusalem
- 9 March: 11 killed and 54 injured in a coffee shop in Jerusalem
- 20 March: seven killed and 30 injured on a bus in northern Israel
- 21 March: three killed and 86 injured in a shopping centre in Jerusalem
- 27 March: 30 killed and 140 injured at a religious feast in Netanya
- 29 March: two killed and 28 injured in a supermarket in Jerusalem
- 31 March: 16 killed and 40 injured in a restaurant in Haifa.

In 16 other separate incidents that month, most of which involved shootings, a further 31 Israelis were killed and 134 injured.

Israelis demanded action. In February 2001, Ariel Sharon was elected prime minister. He promised Israelis 'security and peace' and his response to the new Intifada was hard-line: all attacks were dealt with by force and the use of tear gas and live ammunition; there were mass arrests of suspects and Palestinian leaders were targeted for assassination.

But the wave of Palestinian attacks continued, reaching a climax in 'Black March' of 2002, when suicide bombings, shootings and knife attacks killed 111 Israeli civilians and injured a further 560. Sharon immediately stepped up his response, saying: 'The Palestinians must be hit, and it must be very painful… We must cause them losses, victims, so that they feel a heavy price.'

- He ordered **Operation Defensive Shield**. Israeli troops forcibly reoccupied the six largest Palestinian cities in the West Bank. For 2 months, strict curfews were imposed. 15,000 suspects were arrested; weapons were confiscated; bomb-making equipment was destroyed. 500 Palestinians were killed and 1,500 injured. Particularly fierce fighting took place in the refugee camp of Jenin, where 54 Palestinians and 23 IDF were killed, and thousands made homeless when their houses were destroyed. When the IDF finally withdrew, military **cordons** and checkpoints were left in place to prevent Palestinians from travelling freely.
- Simultaneously, the IDF laid siege to Yasser Arafat's presidential compound in Ramallah, which was bombed so thoroughly that it was ruined. Sharon saw Arafat as corrupt and responsible for terrorism. The siege was only lifted when Arafat was airlifted to France in October 2004 to receive medical treatment.
- Then, in June 2002, Sharon ordered the construction of a massive 'security fence' to keep Palestinian terrorists out of Israel. The first part was completed a year later and, as he had hoped, the number of suicide bombings immediately decreased.

SOURCE J

An online American-based journal describes the impact of Operation Defensive Shield on Palestinian children under the age of 18.

55 children were killed. Thirty-eight percent were under 12 years of age… 24 died from live bullets including rubber-coated metal bullets, 7 from shelling, bombing or explosions, 5 from delays in receiving healthcare, 10 from acts of violence such as beatings or being struck by army vehicles, and 6 were buried under the rubble by a bulldozer… During the third day of the incursion into Nablus, the Shu'bi family home was demolished by an Israeli bulldozer; the mother, seven-months pregnant, and, three brothers, Abdullah, 8, Azzam, 6, and Anas, 4, were buried under the rubble, along with their grandfather and two aunts.

SOURCE K

The difficulties of everyday life. Here a Palestinian family climbs over a wall of cement barricades – erected by Israel to combat suicide bombers – to cross from East Jerusalem to the village of Abu Dis in the West Bank, 18 September 2003.

EXTEND YOUR KNOWLEDGE

THE 'SECURITY FENCE' OR WEST BANK BARRIER

Also called the 'separation wall' by Israelis, the Apartheid Wall by Palestinians and the West Bank Barrier by others, Sharon's security fence is now 708 km long. Most of it consists of a 60-metre (200 foot) wide 'exclusion zone' fortified with high fences, barbed wire and guard posts. In places where Palestinians and Israelis live close together, an 8-metre high wall has been erected. The barrier has made many Israelis feel safer, but it has also made ordinary life for Palestinians extremely difficult. For example, some cannot get to their farmland.

Sharon's campaign achieved results: the number of West Bank terrorist attacks on Israelis fell. But, in other ways, his campaign backfired. The level of damage and number of casualties, including women and children, shocked the international media and hardened Palestinians' hatred for Israel.

Meanwhile, the 'security fence' became a major new source of tension. This was because only some of it was built on Israeli land or followed the 1949 ceasefire lines: most of it cut deeply into Palestinian land. Palestinians (supported by the International Court of Justice) angrily argued that Israel was illegally seizing West Bank land for Jewish settlers.

ACTIVITY

Organise a class debate on Sharon's security fence, with one side arguing in favour and the other side arguing against. Each side will need to do some research, in order to support their argument with exact examples and images.

5.5 AN ATTEMPT TO RESTART THE TALKS: THE ROADMAP FOR PEACE, 2003

LEARNING OBJECTIVES

- Understand why there was a demand for a roadmap
- Understand how and why the Roadmap for Peace failed
- Understand the impact of the Second Intifada on Palestinians and on Israelis.

KEY TERM

Roadmap for Peace an official plan to achieve peace in the future, that sets out what each country, government, group etc. should try to do at particular stages along the way; a phased plan aimed at achieving a particular goal

Increasingly alarmed by the situation, the European Union, the United Nations, the USA and Russia all supported a new proposal known as the **Roadmap for Peace** (see Figure 5.6). Sharon was now in a position of strength: he agreed to talk, but not with Arafat. So, reluctantly, Arafat agreed to appoint Mahmoud Abbas as Palestinian prime minister and spokesman.

EXAM-STYLE QUESTION

AO1 **AO2**

Explain **two** ways in which the Roadmap for Peace (2003) was similar to the Oslo Peace Accords (1993). **(6 marks)**

HINT
You will get one mark for each similarity you identify, one mark for explaining that similarity and one mark for using supporting information.

In June 2003, Sharon and Abbas met with US President Bush: they agreed on the Roadmap in principle; they shook hands and went home. But, within days, the Roadmap looked doomed. Arafat refused to give it his support. The cycle of violence resumed. Frustrated, Abbas resigned.

ATTEMPTS AT LASTING PEACE — THE MIDDLE EAST, 1917–2012

▶ Figure 5.6 The Roadmap for Peace, 2003

Phase 1
- Palestinians to end all violence and hand over weapons
- Israel to freeze all settlement building and pull out from any built since 2000

Phase 2
A conference to be convened to establish a truly democratic and sovereign Palestinian state

Phase 3
Discussions to be held on:
- Jerusalem's status
- Palestinian refugees' right to return

Goal: Peace · A two-state solution

Roadmap for Peace

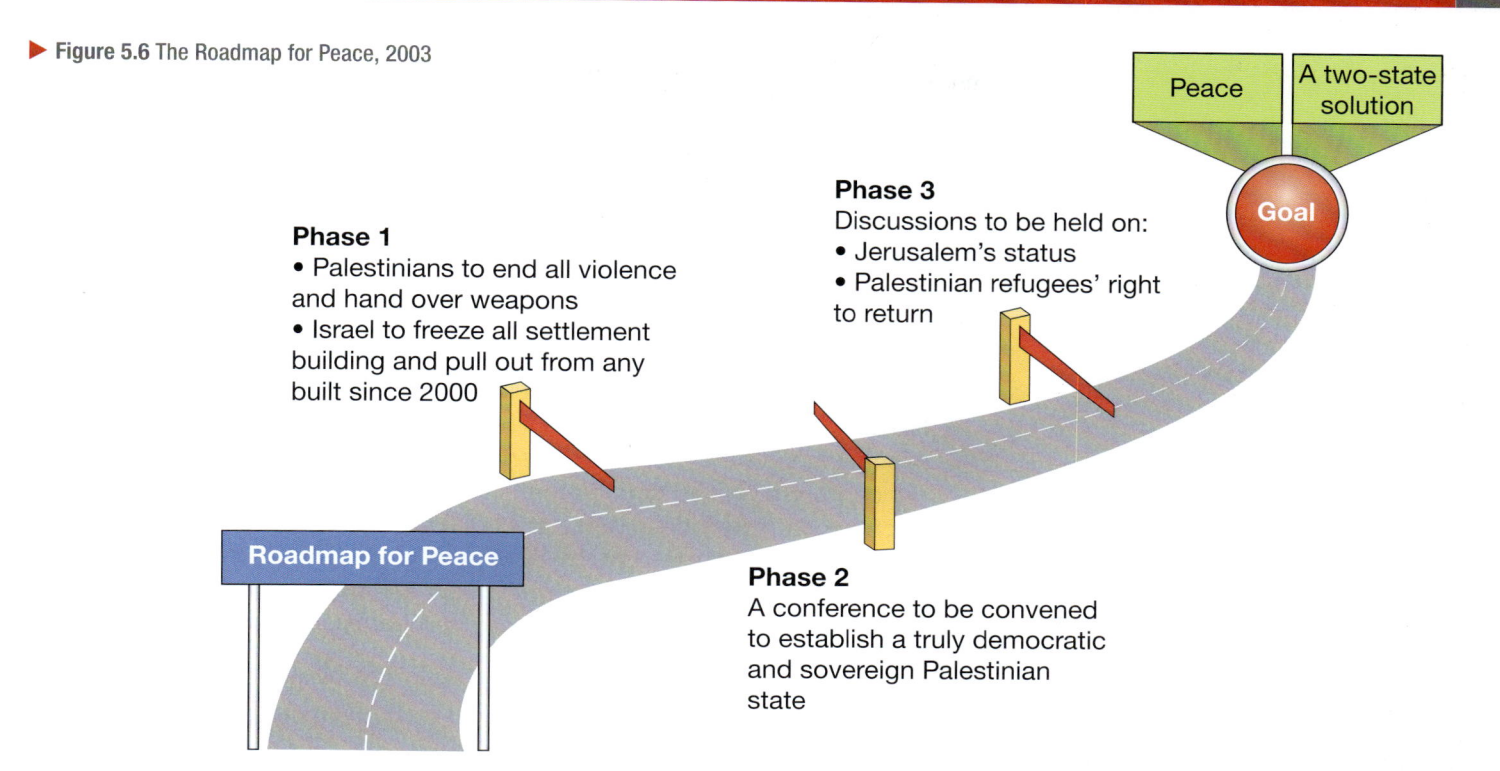

EXTEND YOUR KNOWLEDGE

THE DEATH OF ARAFAT, NOVEMBER 2004

For 30 months, Arafat lived in his besieged compound in Ramallah. Then his health suddenly collapsed. He flew to Paris for treatment, but died from multiple organ failure following a stroke. His funeral was held in Cairo, and then his body was flown back to Ramallah. There, amid a massive crowd of highly emotional, gun-firing mourners, Arafat was buried in the ruins of his old compound.

Many Palestinians believe that Arafat was the victim of an Israeli assassination plot. One theory is that Sharon had him poisoned with polonium-210, a radioactive substance. But when Arafat's body was dug up in 2012 for scientific testing, the results were unclear.

However, the Roadmap did not vanish. Eighteen months later, three events resulted in a year of optimism.

1. In November 2004, Arafat died and, in early January 2005, Mahmoud Abbas was elected president of the Palestinian National Authority. Abbas made a genuine effort to end Palestinian violence against Israel.
2. Impressed by this, Sharon agreed to meet with Abbas and to resume talks on the Roadmap. The meeting was a success: helped by a US promise of $50 million aid, militant Palestinian groups agreed to a ceasefire; Israel agreed to withdraw from the Palestinian towns it had occupied; both sides agreed to exchange prisoners. In February 2005, the Intifada was officially declared to be over.
3. In February 2005, the Israeli Knesset finally agreed that Israel would pull out of the Gaza Strip. This 'Disengagement Plan', as it was called, had been proposed by Sharon in 2003. The plan was very unpopular with many Israelis, but Sharon was under pressure from the USA to improve relations with the Palestinians in return for aid.

By September 2005, the 21 Israeli settlements in Gaza had been dismantled, 8,000 settlers had been relocated and compensated, and the last Israeli soldier had been withdrawn. Though Israel won international praise for pulling out of Gaza, the cost for Sharon was high. He lost support in his own party, and founded a new party called Kadima or 'Forward'.

THE IMPACT OF THE SECOND INTIFADA

So, officially, the Second Intifada ended in February 2005. It had lasted for 4 years and 4 months. It is hard to see what either side gained. Civilian casualties hardened the determination to resist, deepened hatreds and poisoned peacemaking efforts.

THE IMPACT ON PALESTINIANS

- **Casualties**: about 5,000 Palestinians were killed; many thousands more were injured and arrested.
- **Economic damage**: before the Second Intifada, ten per cent of Palestinians were unemployed; by 2005, the level had risen to 25 per cent. Tourism collapsed. For example, before the Intifada, about 92,000 tourists visited Bethlehem every month; in the whole of 2004, only 7,249 visited. By 2005, 60 per cent of Palestinians were living in poverty.
- **Homelessness**: about 5,000 homes were destroyed by the IDF during the Intifada and thousands more were too damaged to live in. In the Gaza town of Rafah, nine per cent of the population lost their homes.
- **Hardship and suffering**: largely built on West Bank territory, Sharon's security fence separated 12 per cent of Palestinians from their farmland; ten per cent were even marooned to the *west* of the barrier. The huge number of **checkpoints** made internal travel difficult.
- **Inconvenience**: for example, during Operation Defensive Shield, PNA ministries were ransacked, and paperwork and computers were destroyed.
- **Negative publicity**: the suicide bombings in particular earned widespread condemnation.

If there was one positive, it was that Sharon ordered the Israeli evacuation of Gaza. However, since Israel still controlled Gaza's airspace, coastline and borders, Gaza was hardly free.

THE IMPACT ON ISRAELIS

- **Casualties**: 1,063 Israelis died, of whom 731 were civilians; 8,800 were wounded.
- **Economic damage**: tourism collapsed, while the cost of military operations was huge; by 2005, ten per cent of Israelis were unemployed and 30 per cent lived in poverty.
- **Psychological damage**: less easy to measure, the Intifada – and especially the suicide bombings – was exceptionally stressful for Israelis. They felt that they were the victims and in the right; the opposition was therefore wrong.
- **Negative publicity**: Israel's harsh tactics and its refusal to follow international law were strongly criticised. It also unintentionally drew world attention to the plight of the Palestinians.

If there was a gain from the Intifada for Israelis, it was an increased level of security. Perhaps this was because of Sharon's fence, but the Palestinian ceasefire also played a role.

EXAM-STYLE QUESTION

A01 **A02**

Explain **two** ways in which the Second Intifada of 2000–05 was different from the First Intifada of 1987–93. **(6 marks)**

> **HINT**
>
> This question is testing your ability to explain differences. To get a good mark, once you have identified a difference, provide some supporting information from each Intifada to prove your point.

ROAD BLOCKS – THE FAILURE OF THE ROADMAP FOR PEACE

Since 2005 was such a year of optimism, there was hope that the Roadmap would now move smoothly to Phase 2. This did not happen.

In January 2006, Sharon suffered a massive stroke. Even if he had remained in power, it is doubtful that progress would have been made. Right-wing Israelis refused to consider withdrawing from the West Bank, where 400,000 Jewish settlers now lived, and refused to surrender even a part of Jerusalem to be the capital of a new Palestinian state. They did not consider the Palestinian point of view, possibly because the security barrier meant that West Bank Palestinians were now 'invisible' to them.

Even more damagingly, Hamas won control of the Palestinian Assembly in the January 2006 elections.

SOURCE L

Writing in December 2016, an Israeli living in Britain describes the impact of the Hamas victory on Israel.

One cannot overestimate the impact of the Hamas win in Gaza on the Israeli public. Israelis saw Gaza as an experiment: "Let's see what happens if we do give up territory." The election of a party calling for the destruction of Israel, following a withdrawal from Gaza, convinced most middle-of-the-road Israelis that the Palestinians do not want to live in peace with Israel. This, in my view, gave a massive boost to the right in Israel and started the final process that brought it to the dominance it enjoys at the moment.

EXTEND YOUR KNOWLEDGE

WHY DID PALESTINIANS VOTE FOR HAMAS?
Despite the huge expression of grief that followed Arafat's death, many Palestinians were frustrated with Fatah. It seemed corrupt and ineffective. In contrast, Hamas put effort into providing social care and facilities.

Hamas opposed peace and its success in the elections meant the peace process ended.

- Hamas wanted the complete destruction of Israel and refused to attend Roadmap talks. Hamas militants in Gaza fired **Qassam rockets** into Israel – perhaps over 1,000 were fired in the first half of 2006 alone. Israel responded to every rocket attack by bombing the launch site in Gaza, and by strengthening its blockade around Gaza to stop Hamas acquiring weapons. Hamas began smuggling bomb-making equipment through tunnels under the border with Egypt.
- Because Hamas refused to cease violence or recognise Israel, the four countries behind the Roadmap saw it as a terrorist organisation and put in place **sanctions** that stopped all foreign aid to the Palestinian National Authority.
- Hamas fiercely opposed Mahmoud Abbas and his party, Fatah. Tension between Fatah and Hamas soon flared into open violence. In June 2007, Fatah attempted to seize control; in response, Hamas expelled all Fatah members from Gaza.

EXTEND YOUR KNOWLEDGE

QASSAM ROCKETS
Qassams were named after a Syrian Imam who led Palestinian resistance against the British Mandate until he was killed in 1935. The simple, homemade rockets were propelled by a mixture of sugar and potassium nitrate (a fertiliser). They could not be aimed, which meant that civilian as well as military targets were hit. That may have been deliberate anyway. Although Qassam attacks disrupted daily life for Israelis living within range and had a psychological impact, they were not very effective. Israel used a radar system to detect incoming rockets. Loudspeakers then warned civilians to take cover. As a result, only about 15 Israelis were killed by Qassams between 2001 and 2008.

5.6 THE GAZA WAR, 2008–09

LEARNING OBJECTIVES

- Understand the causes of the Gaza War
- Understand how Operation Cast Lead began the war
- Understand the impact of the Gaza War on Palestinians and on Israelis.

Life for Palestinians, especially in Gaza, rapidly became worse. Some even called Gaza a 'Hell on Earth'. Israel's blockade and international sanctions meant a lack of food, medical supplies and fuel. Eighty per cent of the population lived in extreme poverty. Civilians were also caught up in the violent struggle between Hamas and Fatah supporters, and fell victim to Israeli airstrikes on Gazan rocket launchers.

The summer of 2008 brought some relief when Egypt negotiated a truce between Israel and Hamas. But neither side saw the truce as permanent. Israel began preparing for a powerful assault on Gaza, aimed at removing the 20,000 armed members of Hamas living there and ending the Qassam rocket attacks. Hamas expected this and so prepared for defensive urban warfare. In December 2008, Hamas announced it was ending the truce.

EXTEND YOUR KNOWLEDGE

WHY DID ISRAEL LAUNCH OPERATION CAST LEAD?
Since Qassam rockets were not very effective, the scale of Operation Cast Lead was surprising. One reason for the attack on Gaza may lie elsewhere. In July 2006, Israel had invaded Lebanon, in an effort to destroy Hezbollah attacks on northern Israel. The attack failed. Israel now needed to make a show of strength to prove, especially to Iran which supported Hezbollah, that it was still a powerful military force. The timing of Israel's attack on Gaza may relate to the fact that Barack Obama won the US presidential election in November 2008. He would not be a friend of Israel in the way that President Bush had been so, if Israel was going to attack Gaza, it had to be before Obama took over in January 2009.

The Gaza War started at 11.30 a.m. on 27 December 2008, when Israel launched Operation Cast Lead. In the first four minutes, Israeli airstrikes hit 100 pre-planned targets in Gaza; half an hour later, a second wave of attacks targeted Hamas headquarters, government offices and 24 police stations. On the first day of the Gaza War, 225 Palestinians died. It was the deadliest day in 60 years of conflict. Palestinians called it the 'Massacre of Black Saturday'. Hamas responded with rocket attacks. On 3 January 2009, the Israeli ground invasion of Gaza began. The aim was to kill Hamas fighters, seize control of Hamas rocket-making equipment and weapons, and destroy the tunnels between Gaza and Egypt through which Hamas smuggled weapons. The conflict lasted for 3 weeks.

EXAM-STYLE QUESTION

A01 A02

SKILLS ADAPTIVE LEARNING

Explain **two** causes of the Gaza War of 2008–09. **(8 marks)**

HINT
This question is testing your ability to explain why an event happened. A good answer would have supporting details. Remember to write about two causes.

| ATTEMPTS AT LASTING PEACE | THE MIDDLE EAST, 1917–2012 | 105 |

SOURCE M

Foreign press gather on a hilltop overlooking the Gaza Strip, 5 January 2009, frustrated by the fact that Israel refused them permission to go any further.

THE EFFECTS OF THE GAZA WAR

The impact of the war on Gaza was shocking: 4,000 homes, 600 factories and businesses, 24 mosques, eight hospitals, plus roads, bridges and many UNRWA facilities were destroyed. Over 1,000 Palestinians were killed, a third of them children. Many more were wounded, casualties of the fact that Hamas used civilians as human shields and fired rockets from urban areas. By the end of the war, most of the battered Gaza population was forced to rely on aid.

In comparison, only 13 Israelis were killed and Israel achieved the tactical victory it had wanted. Hamas lost fighters, weapons and tunnels. The cross-border rocket attacks stopped. But Israel lost the propaganda war. The media was full of images of civilian casualties, and destroyed schools and mosques. Israel was accused of using unnecessary force and illegal weapons like white phosphorus.

ACTIVITY

Look at Sources M and N, and see if you and a partner can answer these two questions.
1 If journalists were banned from Gaza, how did anyone know what was happening inside Gaza? Can you think of five ways that information might have got out?
2 'Protests against Operation Cast Lead took place across the world.' Does Source N support this statement?

SOURCE N

A 'Stop the War' demonstration in Edinburgh, Scotland, 10 January 2009. It was organised to protest against Israeli involvement in Gaza.

Furthermore, any Israeli gains were only short term. Hamas was not significantly weakened, hatred for Israel increased, and the rocket attacks soon restarted. In March 2012, for example, Palestinian militants launched over 300 rockets attacks; Israel responded with a 5-day air assault. So, despite 25 years of attempting to find peace, the two sides remained as far apart in 2012 as they had been in 1987.

ACTIVITY

An event is significant if it has a major impact and results in important consequences. The following events all had a significant impact on attempts at finding a solution to the Arab–Israeli conflict:
- the oil crisis of 1973
- the invasion of Lebanon in 1982
- the First Intifada of 1987–93
- the end of the Cold War and the Gulf War in 1991
- the Second Intifada of 2000–05.

Can you explain, with reasons, which of these had a significant impact on:
- American attitudes to the Arab–Israeli conflict
- the PLO's attitudes to the Arab–Israeli conflict
- Israeli attitudes to the Arab–Israeli conflict.

WHAT WERE THE MOTIVES OF THE KEY PLAYERS IN ATTEMPTS TO FIND PEACE?

YITZAK RABIN

Rabin belonged to the left wing of Israeli politics: he supported negotiating a peace deal with the Palestinians, but felt Israel needed to be in a position of strength to negotiate that deal in its own interests. He believed that the situation in the early 1990s presented the best opportunity for peace in his political career.

BINYAMIN NETANYAHU

Netanyahu believes that Jews have historic rights over the whole of 'Biblical Israel' but probably accepts that this is not practical. He was, therefore, willing to trade *some* land for peace though he would never accept a return to the 1967 borders. To strengthen the Israeli presence in the areas, he encouraged Jewish settlement in the West Bank, even when these settlements were considered illegal by the UN and prolonged the conflict with the Palestinians. He did this to keep the support of ultra ring-wing parties.

HAMAS

At the time of the Gaza War, Hamas regarded the whole of historic Palestine as Islamic land and therefore viewed the state of Israel as an occupier. It did not believe in a negotiated settlement, seeing the PLO as corrupt and betraying Palestinians during the Oslo and Roadmap for Peace negotiations. It justified any actions against Israel, including suicide bombings and rocket attacks, as legitimate resistance. In Gaza, it argued that Israel's blockade justified a counter-attack by any means possible.

HEZBOLLAH

Hezbollah is committed to the destruction of the state of Israel, for several reasons: it believes Israel is an illegal state; it sought revenge for all Israel's operations against and in Lebanon; and it demanded the return of territory occupied by Israel. Funded in part by Iran, Hezbollah is a Shia Muslim organisation and originally aimed to create an Islamic republic in Lebanon.

USA

Since it voted for its creation, the USA has generally supported Israel, initially with food aid and then, from the 1960s, with military aid. This support partly relates to the fact that around 7 million Jews (or about 40 per cent of the world total) live in America, though not all are pro-Israeli. At the height of the Cold War, the USA needed an ally in the area. Finally, US policy had also depended on who was US president. For example, Bill Clinton devoted a great deal of time and energy on pushing both Palestinians and Israelis towards a peace deal; in contrast, George W. Bush closely allied himself with Israel.

RECAP

RECALL QUIZ

1. What was the name given to the Palestinian uprising of 1987–93?
2. What was the 'Iron Fist' policy?
3. What were the dates of: Arafat's speech to the UN renouncing terrorism; the Oslo Peace Accords; Oslo II; the Roadmap for Peace?
4. Which Israeli prime minister agreed to the Oslo Peace Accords?
5. What happened to him?
6. Give two reasons why the Oslo Peace Accords failed.
7. Which event triggered the Second Intifada?
8. Many different Palestinian groups operated during the Second Intifada: name two of them and describe their aims and tactics.
9. Describe three ways in which Sharon responded to the Second Intifada.
10. Who proposed the Roadmap for Peace?
11. Give two reasons why the Roadmap for Peace failed to make progress.
12. Describe two effects of the Gaza War.

CHECKPOINT

STRENGTHEN

- **S1** Explain why Arafat renounced terrorism in 1988.
- **S2** Explain why the Israeli government refused to negotiate with the PLO after Arafat renounced terrorism, but then changed its mind.
- **S3** Draw a diagram that shows how and why international attitudes to the Palestinian issue changed in the years 1987–2009.

CHALLENGE

- **C1** Why did some Israelis object to the Oslo Accords and the Roadmap for Peace?
- **C2** Why did Palestinians object to them?
- **C3** In what ways have the following blocked further peace negotiations between Palestinians and Israel: Jewish settlements in the West Bank; the security fence; rival claims to Jerusalem; Qassam attacks on Israel; Israeli attacks on Gaza?

SUMMARY

- The First Intifada erupted in 1987.
- Yasser Arafat renounced terrorism in a speech to the UN in 1988.
- The end of the Cold War and the Gulf War forced both sides to compromise.
- The PLO and Israel agreed on the Oslo Accords in 1993 and set up the PNA.
- In 1995, Oslo II established which areas would be governed by the PNA.
- The Second Intifada began in 2000.
- Israel responded with Operation Defensive Shield and built a security fence.
- The Roadmap for Peace, 2003, was an attempt to restart peace talks.
- It resulted in an end to the Second Intifada and Israel's withdrawal from Gaza, but made no further progress.
- Qassam rocket attacks on southern Israel resulted in the Gaza War of 2008–09.

ATTEMPTS AT LASTING PEACE   THE MIDDLE EAST, 1917–2012   109

EXAM GUIDANCE: PART (C) QUESTIONS

A01 **A02**

SKILLS PROBLEM SOLVING, REASONING, DECISION MAKING

Questions to be answered: How far was the USA responsible for peace initiatives in the Middle East in the period 1974–2005?

You may use the following in your answer:
- **Camp David Accords, 1978**
- **Roadmap for Peace, 2003.**

You must also use information of your own. (16 marks)

1 **Analysis Question 1: What is the question type testing?**
In this question you have to demonstrate that you have knowledge and understanding of the key features and characteristics of the period studied. In this particular case it is knowledge and understanding of the role of the USA in peace initiatives in the period 1974–2005.

You also have to explain, analyse and make judgements about historical events and periods to give an explanation and reach a judgement on the role of various factors in bringing about changes.

2 **Analysis Question 2: What do I have to do to answer the question well?**
- You have been given two factors on which to write. You don't have to use those factors (though it might be wise to do so). You must, however, include at least one extra factor, other than those you have been given.
- That factor might be Henry Kissinger's 'shuttle diplomacy', the evacuation of the PLO from Beirut or the Oslo Peace Accords.
- But you must avoid just describing them. Explain what changes resulted from these peace initiatives.
- You are also asked 'how far' the USA was responsible for the change. So, when discussing these events, you need to consider whether it was the USA that was causing the peace initiatives to happen or whether there were other factors that might have caused those peace initiatives.
- Don't write a lengthy introduction. Give a brief one, which answers the question straight away and shows what your paragraphs are going to be about.
- Make sure you stay focused on the question and avoid just writing narrative, try to use the words of the question at the beginning of each paragraph.
- Remember this question is a causation question, so make sure what you are writing about explains why this did or did not mean the USA caused change.

Answer
Here is a student response with teacher comments.

These years saw some very important peace initiatives, and the USA played a role in many of these. For example, in 1974 Henry Kissinger used 'shuttle diplomacy' to persuade Israel, Egypt and Syria to move towards better relations. That brought about peace along the Suez Canal, so it could be cleared and reopened for trade. In 1978, US President Jimmy Carter stepped in when peace talks between Egypt and Israel slowed down. He invited Sadat and Begin for talks at Camp David, and without his intervention the Washington Peace Treaty (which resulted in peace between Israel and Egypt) might not have happened. The USA also played a role in evacuating the PLO from Beirut in 1982 and ending the Israeli seige of Beirut. In the 1990s, the USA put pressure on Israel to negotiate with the PLO, by threatening to withhold financial aid, helping to bring about the Oslo Accords. Finally, the USA also played a role in proposing the Roadmap for Peace in 2004 and in helping to end the Second Intifada. By promising $50 million aid, militant Palestinian groups agreed to a ceasefire.

However, the USA's role in some of these peace initiatives must not be overstated. Firstly, other powers were also involved. For example, the UN also played a very important role in peacemaking when it invited Arafat to speak to it. The Madrid Peace Conference of 1991 was proposed jointly by the USSR and the USA, and backed by Middle Eastern states like Saudi Arabia. That peace conference almost came to nothing and the Oslo Peace Accords might not have happened at all except for the negotiating skills of the Norwegian Foreign Minister. Meanwhile, the EU, the UN and Russia were also behind the Roadmap for Peace. It was not just a US initiative.

Also some peace initiatives came about because of changing attitudes among Israelis and Palestinians. One of the reasons Israel agreed to negotiations with the PLO was because it needed to end the First Intifada, and because it was concerned by the rise of Hamas. Arafat needed a settlement with Israel because he had lost his key supporter when the USSR collapsed, and lost Middle East backers like Kuwait and Saudi Arabia when he supported Saddam Hussein. So, it was not just US pressure that made them negotiate. Palestinian militant groups agreed to the ceasefire in 2005 because Sharon's security barrier made it increasingly difficult for them to run suicide bomb missions. It was not just the promise of US aid.

So the USA played a key role in the peace initiatives in the 1970s, but after that, other factors, such as the UN, the EU and the changing attitudes of the Israelis and Palestinians were very important.

Teacher comments

Where is your introduction? What is missing is a short overview of the whole answer. This could be achieved by looking at the opening sentences of each of the paragraphs below: together they should add up to an overview.

This is a great paragraph. It has an opening sentence that explains what the paragraph is about – the point of the paragraph – and it then uses detailed knowledge to support the point. And you are using extra knowledge! Well done.

Another good paragraph. You answer the question, give contextual knowledge and link peace initiatives to powers other than the USA. So, you are really addressing the 'How far…' part of the question. However, a touch more is sometimes needed. For example: Arafat's speech to the UN – which one? What date was it? What impact did that have on the peace process?

Another very good opening sentence, where you referred back to the words of the question to keep it all relevant. You could be even more exact with your detail. For example, when you said 'some peace initiatives', which were you referring to?

Good – a concise finish, which shows change over time and makes it clear where the USA played a role.

Work with a friend
Discuss how you would create an introduction to get very high marks. Does your answer do the following?

- ☐ Identify areas of US involvement in peacemaking initiatives
- ☐ Provide detailed information to support those
- ☐ Show how US involvement led to the given outcome
- ☐ Provide at least one factor other than those given in the question
- ☐ Address 'how far?'

GLOSSARY

abstain choose not to vote

alliance a group of countries working together

anti-Semitism a dislike for or hatred of Jews

artillery large guns, either on wheels or fixed in one place

assimilate to absorb and integrate. In this case, immigrants were absorbed and integrated into Israeli society and culture

atrocities horrrifying and violent actions, especially during a war

backfired if a plan or action backfires, it has the opposite effect to the one you intended

besieged surrounded and unable to leave

boycott to refuse to buy something, use something, or take part in something as a way of protesting; the refusal to co-operate or participate in something. When people refuse to buy goods as a punishment or protest against something, they are boycotting those goods

censorship to examine books, films, letters etc. and remove anything that is considered politically dangerous

checkpoint a place, especially on a border, where an official person examines vehicles or people

cordon a line of police officers, soldiers, or vehicles that is put around an area to stop people going there

crucify/ied / crucifixion to kill someone by fastening them to a cross and leaving them to die

crusader Christian soldier who took part in the Crusades, a series of wars fought in the 11th, 12th and 13th centuries by Christian armies

curfew a law that forces people to stay indoors at particular times

deadlock a situation in which a disagreement cannot be settled

descendants people who are all related to someone who lived a long time ago

deter/ deterrent to stop someone from doing something, by making them realise it will be difficult or have bad results

embargo an official order to stop trade with another country

escalate if a bad situation escalates, it becomes much worse

ghettoes areas of a city, often the poorest and most run down, given over to a minority group, in this case, Jews

guerrilla a member of a small unofficial military group that fights in small groups; fighters who use methods of warfare like sabotage, ambushes, raids, and 'hit-and-run' tactics

hijack to use violence or threats to take control of a plane, vehicle, or ship

Holocaust the killing of millions of Jews and other people by the Nazis during the Second World War

Holy Land the parts of the Middle East where most of the events mentioned in the Bible happened

infiltrate to secretly enter a place, sometimes in order to harm it

inflation a continuing increase in prices

infra-red infra-red light gives out heat but cannot be seen

insurgency a rebellion – an attempt by a group of people to take control of their government using force and violence

Intifada Arabic word meaning 'shaking off'. In this case it refers to the Palestinian rebellion of 1987–93 that sought to 'shake off' Israeli control of the occupied territories. The goal was independence

irrigation (irrigate) to supply land or crops with water

mobilise (v) if a country mobilises or mobilises its army, it prepares to fight a war

Nazism the policies of the National Socialist Party of Adolf Hitler, which controlled Germany from 1933 to 1945

offensive (attack) a planned military attack

Operation Defensive Shield Israeli reoccupation of the six largest Palestinian cities in the West Bank, in retaliation for Black March

outrage / outraged a feeling of great anger and shock

partition to divide. In this case, the word is used to refer to the division of Palestine into Arab and Jewish territories

peace initiative a plan to make peace

peace treaty a formal written agreement between two or more countries or governments to stop fighting

peasant a poor farmer who owns or rents a small amount of land

persecution ill-treatment, especially because of race or political or religious beliefs

playboy a rich man who does not work and who spends his time enjoying himself with beautiful women, fast cars etc.

propaganda information which is false or which emphasises just one part of a situation, used by a government or political group to make people agree with them

Promised Land Jewish phrase for the land of Canaan, which was promised by God to Abraham and his people in the Bible

GLOSSARY

Qassam rockets simple, homemade rockets that could not be aimed

reprisal a violent or harmful action taken to punish someone for something bad they have done to you; acts of revenge and retaliation

retaliate / retaliation to do something bad to someone because they have done something bad to you

riot a situation in which a large crowd of people are behaving in a violent and uncontrolled way, especially when they are protesting about something

sabotage to deliberately spoil someone's plans because you do not want them to succeed

sanctions official orders or laws stopping trade, communication etc with another country, as a way of forcing its leaders to make political changes

shuttle diplomacy international talks in which someone travels between countries and talks to members of the governments, for example to make a peace agreement

sniper someone who shoots at people from a hidden position

superpowers nations that have very great military and political power, like the USA and Soviet Union in the Cold War

suppression to stop people from opposing the government, especially by using force

synagogue a building where Jewish people meet for religious worship

traitor someone who is not loyal to their country or their beliefs

triumph / triumphal a victory or success gained after a difficult struggle

truce an agreement between enemies to stop fighting for a specified length of time

uprising an attempt by a group of people to change the government or laws

war of attrition a struggle in which you wear your enemy down

withdrawal / withdraw the act of moving an army, weapons, etc. away from the area where they were fighting

Zionist someone who supports the establishment and development of a state for the Jews in Israel

INDEX

A
Abbas, Mahmoud 100–1, 103
al-Aqsa Martyrs' Brigade 98
al-Bassa massacre 9
al-Nakba 28, 32
anti-Semitism 4, 7, 17, 30, 32
Arab League 29, 33, 72, 75
Arab nationalism 4, 34, 36
Arab Revolt 6, 9
Arab Strike 6, 8
Arab–Israeli War (1948–49) 25–30
    see also Dogfight (1967); Gaza War; Samu Raid; Six Day War; War of Attrition; Yom Kippur War
Arafat, Yasser 45–6, 56–7, 58, 59, 77, 78, 79, 91–3, 100, 101
    Oslo Accords 93–4, 96
    Second Intifada 98, 99
    UN speeches 72–3, 89–90
armistice agreements 26
Assad, President 62, 71
assimilation 32
Aswan Dam 33, 34, 35, 37, 38, 39, 40, 53

B
Balfour Declaration 2, 5–6
Bar Lev Line 60, 61, 63, 64
Begin, Menachem 12, 13, 20, 73–6, 78, 97
Beirut 58, 77, 79
Ben-Gurion, David 7, 9, 24, 25, 26, 27, 32, 35, 36
Bernadotte, Count 26
Bevin, Ernest 11, 15
Black March 99
Black September 58, 76
Black September Organisation 58–9
blockades 13, 35, 36, 37, 103, 104, 107
boycotts 8, 16, 33, 86, 88, 96
Britain 2, 5–6, 24, 33, 34, 35–7, 38
British Mandate 6–15, 17–18, 19, 25
buffer zones 54, 55, 78
Bush, George 100, 104, 107

C
Cairo Conference 44–5
Camp David Accords 74–5
Carter, Jimmy 73–6
Clinton, Bill 94, 95, 97, 107
Coastal Road Massacre 78, 79
Cold War 19, 34, 39, 70, 91–2, 107
Cyprus 13
Czechoslovakia 26, 31, 33, 35, 39

D
Dawson's Field 57, 58
Dayan, Moshe 36, 49, 51, 64
Deir Yassin 20, 30
demilitarised zones (DMZs) 47, 71
Diaspora 3
Disengagement Plan 101
Dogfight (1967) 47
Dreyfus, Alfred 4
Druze 77

E
Egypt 24, 33–9, 71, 73–6
    Arab–Israeli War (1948–49) 25–26, 28, 29, 30
    Six Day War 44–5, 47–8, 49–55, 56
    Yom Kippur War 43, 59–65
Eisenhower, Dwight 37
Eshkol, Levi 46, 47, 49
ethnic cleansing 20
exam guidance 22–3, 41–2, 67–8, 82–3, 109–10
Exodus (SS) 13–14

F
Farouk, King 33–34
Fatah 44, 45–6, 47, 56–8, 77, 78, 79, 103
Fedayeen 29, 33, 35, 37, 54, 56
First Intifada 84, 86–9
Framework for Egyptian-Israeli peace / Framework for Peace in the Middle East 74–75
France 5, 24, 35–7, 38, 39, 45, 71, 79

G
Gaza 28, 29, 84, 85, 101, 102, 103
    Oslo Accords 94, 96
    Six Day War 50, 52, 53, 54, 55
    Suez Crisis 33, 35, 36, 37
Gaza War (2008–09) 104–6
Gemayel, Bachir 79
Golan Heights 47, 50, 51, 53, 54–5, 60, 61, 65
guerrilla groups 43, 45, 56–7, 80, 98
Gulf War 90–1, 92

H
Habash, George 56, 57
Haganah 6, 7, 9, 10, 11–14, 20, 25, 26, 32
Hamas 84, 89, 92, 95, 96, 97, 103, 104–6, 107
Headwater Diversion Plan 44, 45
Herzl, Theodor 4, 25
Hezbollah 80, 98, 104, 107
Holocaust 10–11, 14, 15, 16, 19, 27, 30, 32
Holst, Johan Jorgen 93, 94
Hussein, King 46, 47, 58, 59, 61, 76, 89, 95
Hussein, Saddam 91

I
IDF 32, 35, 36, 37, 43, 46, 49–50, 61, 88, 99
Intifada 84, 86–9, 97–100, 101–2
Iran 76, 77, 80, 91, 98, 104, 107
Iraq 8, 25, 26, 28, 31, 32, 48, 90–1
Irgun 8, 10, 11–13, 17–18, 19, 20, 26
'Iron Fist' policy 87, 89
Islamic Jihad 89, 90, 95, 96, 98
Israel 30–2, 36–8, 39, 59, 78–80, 90, 91, 92
    see also Arab–Israeli wars; IDF; Intifada; Jerusalem; peace talks; Suez Crisis

J
Jerusalem 3, 12–13, 16, 20, 29, 50, 53, 54, 90, 103
Jewish Agency 7, 13
Jewish settlements (by 1945) 7, 11, 17
Jewish settlers 85, 88, 89, 92, 95, 96, 97
Jordan 29, 46–8, 55–6, 57, 58, 89
    Arab–Israeli War (1948–49) 25, 26, 27, 28, 30
    Six Day War 50, 51, 54

INDEX

K
Karameh, 57
Khartoum Conference 55
King David Hotel 12–13
Kissinger, Henry 71
Knesset 30, 54, 73, 78, 101
Kuwait 90–1

L
Law of Return 30–2
Lebanon 25, 26, 28, 29, 31, 44, 56, 58, 76–80
Lehi 10, 11–12, 19, 20, 26

M
McMahon-Hussein Agreement 5
Meir, Golda 55, 59, 60, 61, 64
Mossad 32, 59, 61
Mubarak, President 95
Munich Olympics 58, 59, 60

N
Nasser, Gamal Abdel 33, 34–7, 38–9, 44, 47–9, 51, 52–3, 55, 58, 59
Nazism 7, 10
Negev Desert 17, 18, 26
Netanyahu, Benjamin 97, 107
Nobel Peace Prize 75, 94

O
Obama, Barack 104
occupied territories 53–6, 79, 85–9, 99, 101
oil (oil weapon) 5, 10, 11, 52, 55, 63, 65, 70
OPEC 70, 71
Operation Agatha 13
Operation Cast Lead 104
Operation Defensive Shield 99, 102
Operation Litani 78
Operation Peace for Galilee 79–80
Operation Wrath of God 59
Oslo Accords (1993) 93–4
Oslo II Accords (1995) 94–7
Ottoman Empire 4, 5

P
Palestine Civil War 2, 19–20
Partition Plan 2, 16–19
peace talks 71, 73–6, 89–97, 100–3, 107

Peel Commission (Plan) 8–9, 10
Peres, Shimon 97
PFLP 56, 57, 58, 59, 95, 96, 98
Phalange Party 77, 79
PLA 44, 45
Plan Dalet (D) 20, 28
plane hijackings 57, 58, 97
PLO 44, 45, 58, 72–3, 76–80, 89–94
PNA 93, 94–5, 96
pre-emptive strikes 50

Q
Qassam rockets 103, 104

R
Rabin, Yitzhak 71, 92–4, 95, 107
refugees
    Jewish 13–14, 15, 16
    Palestinian 27–8, 29, 43, 44, 55–6, 57, 58, 76–7, 79, 85
reprisal attacks 17, 19–20, 29, 35, 45, 59, 77, 78, 81
'right to return' (Palestinian) 28, 29, 101
Roadmap for Peace 100–1, 103

S
Sabra / Shatila massacres 79, 80
Sadat, Anwar 59–60, 62, 64, 71, 72, 73–6
Salameh, Ali Hassan 59
Samu raid 46–7
Saudi Arabia 11, 29, 44, 70, 91, 92
Second Intifada 84, 97–100, 101–2
Secretary of State 69, 71
Sergeants Affair 17–18
Sèvres Agreement 36
Shamir, Prime Minister 87
Sharm el Sheik 33, 36, 37
Sharon, Ariel 62, 79, 80, 97, 99–100, 101, 103
shuttle diplomacy 71
Sinai 45, 47–55, 60–1, 62, 71
Six Day War 43, 44–5, 49–55, 56, 72, 85, 97
Soviet Union *see* USSR
Straits of Tiran 33, 35, 37, 48, 49, 51, 54, 74
Suez Canal 5, 49, 50, 52–3, 55, 59, 60–4, 66, 71–2, 97
Suez Crisis 24, 33–9
Sykes-Picot Agreement 5
Syria 39, 44–6, 55, 60–5, 71, 77

Arab–Israeli War (1948–49) 25, 26, 28, 29
Six Day War 47–50, 51, 54

T
terrorism 43, 45, 56–59, 72, 78, 89–90, 96, 100
    see also Fedayeen; Hamas; Irgun; Islamic Jihad; Lehi; PFLP
Transjordan Arab Legion 26
Treaty of Washington 75
Truman, Harry 15, 19
Tunisia 31, 79, 91

U
United Arab Republic (UAR) 39, 44
United Nations (UN) 2, 15, 16–19, 26, 29, 63, 72–3, 75, 89–90, 105
    peacekeeping 37, 38, 45, 47, 48, 51, 71, 78
    Resolution 181 19
    Resolution 242 55
UNLU 86, 89
UNRWA 29, 105
UNSCOP 16
USA 15, 19, 38, 55, 90, 91, 92
    diplomacy 70–1, 74–6, 94, 100–1
    and Egypt 34, 35, 36, 39, 60
    and Israel 25, 26, 45, 49, 51, 53, 61, 62, 107
    oil crisis 63, 65, 70
USSR 19, 25, 55, 78, 91–2
    aids Egypt / Syria 35, 37, 38, 39, 47, 53, 61–3

W
Wailing Wall 3, 25, 53, 54
War of Attrition 52–3, 55, 59, 66, 97
West Bank 25, 27, 46–7, 50, 53, 54–5, 63, 65, 94–5, 96
    security fence 99–100, 102, 103
    see also Intifada
white phosphorus shells 80, 105

Y
Yad Mordechai 25
Yemen 31–2
Yom Kippur War 43, 59–65, 70, 76, 97

Z
Zionism 4, 5–6, 7, 11–15, 17, 32